Allah Is Dead

Why Islam is Not a Religion

by
Rebecca Bynum

NEW ENGLISH REVIEW PRESS
newenglishreview.org

New English Review Press

Published by New English Review Press
a subsidiary of World Encounter Institute
PO Box 158397
Nashville, Tennessee 37215

Printed in the United States of America

Cover Design by Kendra Adams

ISBN 978-0-578-07390-3

Second Prinitng

Contents

Acknowledgments

I would like to thank all my colleagues at New English Review who have stuck with me through thick and thin. I would especially like to thank Hugh Fitzgerald, Jerry Gordon, Anthony Daniels (writing as Theodore Dalrymple), Mary Jackson, Esmerelda Weatherwax, Julia Raffety, Norman Berdichevsky, Artemis Gordon Glidden, John M. Joyce, Ares Demertzis, Nidra Poller, Ibn Warraq, Richard L. Rubenstein, Mark Anthony Signorelli, Thomas J. Scheff, Geoffrey Clarfield, David Hamilton, Thomas Ország-Land, Christina McIntosh, Kendra and DL Adams and all the rest of our many contributors whose work gives light and life to our wonderful publication. It is an honor to work with such talented people. I also want to thank our anonymous contributor who has selflessly carried the financial responsibility for many years.

I would especially like to thank my husband, Hal, whose love and unflagging support has given me the courage to continue and has meant more to me than he will ever know.

As therefore the state of man now is, what wisdom can there be to choose, what continence to forbear without the knowledge of evil?... I cannot praise a fugitive and cloistered virtue, unexercised and unbreathed, that never sallies out and sees her adversary, but slinks out of the race where the immortal garland is to be run for, not without dust and heat.

-- John Milton

Introduction

The great argument of the twenty first century is a continuation of a very old argument concerning the nature of reality and its forms, but today we are also facing a fantastic argument about the nature of words, their definitions and the reality they describe. In this book, I take a highly focused look at Islam and whether or not it should rightly be classified or described as a religion, let alone an "Abrahamic religion" or one of the "world's great religions" as it has been presented.

There is no question, of course, that Muslims themselves believe Islam to be a religion. And there is equally no question that Islam harnesses the religious impulse. But it can be argued that communism and Nazism likewise harnessed the religious impulse and that millions of people believed in those ideologies with full religious fervor and devotion. The fact of faith alone does not confer the status of religion on an ideology.

Furthermore, when Islam is analyzed philosophically it reveals itself to be much closer to ideologies such as material determinism, nihilism and even social Darwinism than it is to either Christianity or Judaism. It seems to me that Islam lies on the other side of nihilism from Christianity and the other religions and its morality is inverted - matter is elevated over value. In that sense, it could be termed anti-religion.

When proponents of unlimited mosque construction, for example, cite freedom of religion as their rallying cry, they are forgetting that individual liberty must be balanced by consideration for the welfare of society as a whole. The Constitution protects freedom of religion within certain bounds, but to date there has been no Constitutional definition of what actually constitutes a religion for this purpose. The Founders clearly meant to define religion in a Judeo-Christian context and America has limited religious practices in the past.

An important precedent was set when Utah was threatened with invasion and federal occupation unless the Mormons living there changed their religious practice of polygamy. Because the Church of Jesus Christ of Latter Day Saints had a living prophet who could alter the religious tenets of the Church, essentially assigning polygamy to the afterlife, this change was made possible and Utah entered the Union after polygamy was officially banned in the territory. The Mormon Church now has protection under the religious liberty clause, but it did not while the church sanctioned and its members practiced polygamy.

It must be acknowledged that the nuclear family is the fundamental structural unit of our civilization and has perhaps been the single social element most conducive to individual happiness and fulfillment. Polygamy is not marriage and should never be allowed protection under the idea of freedom of religion. There is little chance, however, that Islam will be changed to allow it to fit in with normal Western customs the way Mormonism was changed. A brochure distributed by the Islamic Center of Murfreesboro, Tennessee, extols the supremacy of polygamy throughout, offering it as a superior lifestyle choice, but nowhere does it even mention that polygamy is illegal in America. It openly advocates breaking the law.

Concerning the definition of religion for First Amendment purposes, many factors need to be taken into account and compared with the Judeo-Christian religious tradition for which the First Amendment was intended. The Internal Revenue Service has a list of rules on what constitutes a religion for tax purposes and by those criteria, Islam qualifies as a religion. In general, however, the courts have avoided trying to define religion so as not to pass judgment on the merits of a creed. Doing so could possibly constitute "establishment" of what religion is and is not, which might be a breech of the Constitution in itself. Therefore to date, the courts have been deliberately vague on the issue of what constitutes religion for the purposes of the First Amendment, but it is doubtful that state of affairs will continue given the general decline of the older Christian congregations and rise of all manner of new isms, ologies and belief systems like Islam. The days when the courts could assume that religions would fall within certain parameters are over.

Religion as we have known it has been good for society. It has nurtured morality, strengthened the family, fostered public service and encouraged social harmony. Islam, on the other hand, is self-segregating, fosters ideas of Muslim supremacy and thereby sows seeds of social discord. Even its tradition of charitable giving is solely for the benefit of fellow Muslims and it utterly destroys the family through its adoption of polygamy.

In addition, Islam is the only religion that requires territorial sovereignty – its laws are laws of the land rather than laws of the heart as we are accustomed to finding in religion. In the Western tradition, legality and morality are two different things. In Islam, they are one and the same. And as Muslims press for their laws to become laws of the land, especially by suppressing criticism of Islam, the clash between these two systems of thought will intensify.

There is, however, a current of modern thought seeking to elevate a laudable personal virtue, that of tolerance, over the greater principle of justice. Is it just to tolerate polygamy in the name of religious freedom? The Supreme Court unanimously ruled in 1878, Reynolds v. United States, it is not. Is it just to tolerate the unequal right to inheritance for women? Is it just to tolerate forced marriage? Is it just to tolerate antisemitism? Is it just to tolerate the preaching of hatred toward non-Muslims? Is it just to tolerate the teaching that Muslims are superior to non-Muslims and that men are superior to women? Is it just to tolerate a parallel legal system based on inequality? There are things that our society cannot tolerate and expect to survive. Justice must take its rightful place above tolerance.

If Islam could be reclassified as primarily a social and political ideology, then the Western world would have a powerful tool with which to deal with its spread and could begin the process of containment in the same way the West contained communism, which in the end, seems to be the only realistic option before us with regard to Islam.

If, however, Islam continues to be classified as a religion and given the full protection and benefits religions receive in America, then we will be helpless to contain it and it will grow and spread without limit in Africa, Western Europe and our United States. Though Islam has many religious aspects, many so primitive they have hardly been recognized for what they are, Islam has to be taken as a whole and classified as an entire belief-system.

In fact, I believe Islam to be the duck-billed platypus of belief systems, not all one thing and not all another. It is a combination of religion and politics and one part cannot be separated from the other. That is why Islam cannot remain in the religion category. It must be recognized for what it is.

Of course, Islam is not the only threat to Western civilization and part of the defense of the West must take the form of revitalization of Western ideals including the belief in transcendent value. I have endeavored to offer some analysis and suggestions in this regard as well, particularly on how Jews and Christians might form a closer ideological alliance. Certainly no one will agree with everything in these pages, but certainly the debate needs to take place.

What is Islam and what, if anything, should we do about it?

1
Form and Fetish

Perhaps never before in the history of the world has there been such a need to dissever living spiritual values from the dead forms, doctrine and dogmas in which they are now imprisoned, dogmas which may have smothered whatever original spiritual thought they may once have contained, dogmas which mistake conformity for righteousness, and living faith for the intellectual consent to believe in a doctrine. Islam, for all its faults, is certainly not the only belief system to make this mistake.

Islam does, however, exhibit a consistent tendency to elevate the material over the spiritual and it reduces spiritual reality to a doctrine alone, creating a closed system based in materialism. This system in turn serves to separate the individual from the world of value (the pursuit of value is the purpose of religion) and focuses his mind on the material world alone. An illustration of this is revealed in the attitude of a would-be female suicide bomber's family interviewed by Kevin Toolis for England's Channel 4:

> "'If I had known what Ayat was planning I would have told the Jews. I would have stopped her,' said Ahmed Kmeil, her father.
>
> 'In our religion it is forbidden for a girl's body to be uncovered even at home. How could a girl allow her body to be smashed to pieces and then collected up by Jews? This is absolutely forbidden.'
>
> Even Manal's family insisted that female suicide bombing is wrong. [*Manal was the female recruiter.*]
>
> 'With a man it's different. For us, a girl can't show her leg or

wear a short T-shirt. How can you then be a good Muslim woman and expose your body to the world? What Manal was doing recruiting those girls was wrong,' said her mother Nadia Saba'na.

But what was shocking was none of the families of the would-be female suicide bombers expressed outrage about the innocent civilians their daughters would have killed. They did not seem to be particularly concerned about their daughter's death. What they were worried about was pieces of their daughter's body being exposed to strangers, or worse still, to Jews. They saw everything through this false prism of 'honour'." [1]

And so morality is reduced to a question of material purity. Jews and other infidels are considered to be "unclean" on the same level as urine and feces. If Jews collect the body parts they are thought to "defile" them. The greater moral level, the question of mass murder and suicide, which Westerners perceive at once, is denied to these people whose world view is focused on the material, the world of halal and haram, alone. Islam drives a wedge of materialism between the believer and the greater world of value and morality. Its God is dead.

The tendency toward goodness which we may refer to in general terms as the "will of God" can never be fully contained within a book, holy or otherwise, or within a code, honorable or not, or even within reason itself, for this tendency is a living, changing reality. It is dynamic and adaptive; sought, but never captured; experienced, but never completely known. Traditionally, the independent and transcendent values of truth, beauty and goodness formed the inner yardstick by which value has been measured in the outer world. Truth was the measure of a man, not visa versa.

Radical secularism has also elevated the material above the spiritual and according to this doctrine, man himself has become the measure of all things, and his reasoning power alone is thought to be sufficient in determining good and evil. Religion, when it is considered at all, is assumed to consist of interchangeable, comforting fairy tales

---

1 Toolis, Kevin "Face to face with the women suicide bombers" *The Daily Mail* Feb. 7, 2009

essentially based on man's own inherent goodness. The transcendental, far from being independent, is thought to be completely dependant upon man's own sensibilities and judgment. The only comfort derived from religion is the thought that few really believe in it anyway. Traditional morality is thought, at best, to be an expression of some underlying hypocrisy.

By the light of this secularist viewpoint, modern man draws comfort by imagining himself at the pinnacle of human striving and also by imagining that progress is inevitable. Thus, we feel under no obligation to protect civilization, much less to define it in terms of transcendent value. In the secular world, it has also been thought safe to proclaim, "It doesn't matter what you believe in." Yet what a man believes determines his intention and a man's intention is arguably *the* most important thing for others to know about him.

It is likewise a great mistake to interchange faith and religion semantically as is the current fashion. This leads to mistaking religious dogma for the living experience of faith and may compound the error by forcing uniformity in thought and action and, in the case of the Islamic creed, censoring and even seeking to erase individuality itself. Those who attempt to control faith by enclosing it in form and ritual, only succeed in stifling and eventually killing it, sometimes quickly, sometimes very slowly over centuries.

For example, we know that by the first century, after having existed for roughly two thousand years, Judaism had become moribund and its believers enslaved to tradition and ritual. In the intervening millennia, however, Judaism has evolved and adapted to modern society. Much of this flexibility is derived from a Rabbinic principle that has operated since roughly the year 226 AD known as Dina d'malchuta Dina: the law of the country is binding and, in cases of conflict, to be preferred to Jewish law. [2]

Islam, though the youngest of the world's major belief systems, is in much worse shape today. Islam is entirely regressive and is, in fact, steeped in fetishism and taboo, the oldest religious archetypes, as well as being dominated and defined by gross materialism.

Take for instance the Qur'an, which may well be considered a

---

2 Hausman, Rabbi Jon, "Halacha, Sharia and the Religious Acceptance of Constitutional Governance," *New English Review*, October 2009

fetish book. It is revered not so much for any inspiration it may or may not contain, intended to ennoble the human heart and uplift human morality; rather, it is fetishized as an object. Its verses are considered sacred not on the basis of their power in leading men to goodness, for this outcome is debatable, but simply because they are part of a collective fetish. The value of the Qur'an is the Qur'an itself as a sacred object. Thus the notion of desecration becomes a sure cause for violence, while any expressed doubt by Muslims concerning the veracity of the Qur'an quickly rises to the notion of blasphemy, which under Islam is an offense punishable by death. Hope for reform of Islam in this situation is slender, not least because it would involve the destruction of the Qur'anic fetish, which is at the heart of the system of Islam. This is why the work of scholars like Ibn Warraq is so important; it aims at the de-sacralization of the Qur'an by placing it into its true historic context. The Bible, by contrast may be considered holy, but it is generally understood to be the product of history. It is not thought to contain all truth and has escaped crystallization as a fetish in the minds of believers, "word of God" appellation notwithstanding.

Consider also the black stone located in the Ka'aba in Mecca, which is another major focus of the Muslim religious impulse. This particular meteoric rock also rises to the status of fetish. Muslim prayers are directed toward it, and of course the prayers themselves are fixed forms. Individuality is quashed even during what in the West is considered that most personal of acts; the act of prayer. Neither can it be insignificant that Muslim prayers are literally directed toward a material object.

Islam is set squarely in opposition to living, changing, intangible reality and is also overwhelmingly hostile to natural human affections, for at bottom, it denies the value of love. For Muslims, Islam itself is the highest value, love is hardly considered; and much less consideration is given to the concepts of truth, beauty and goodness which, as transcendent values, are quite simply absent from the Islamic theological scene. By Islam, these values are either ignored or explicitly denied. Though, when pressed, Muslims will tell you all truth is contained within the Qur'an and even, incredibly, that there is no truth outside it. Therefore, it is accurate to say, Islam is a belief system that denies the reality of spirit for Islam recognizes no value higher than itself.

The focus of Islam is entirely upon the material world. It's notions of pure and impure are expressly material as is its concept of religious sovereignty. Islamic sovereignty is territorial sovereignty, not the sovereignty of the spirit over the hearts of men. Islam is totally tied to territorial expansion – the spread of Islamic law – "God's law" over God's land and over the people inhabiting that land who are forced to submit to Islam in a purely material way. Islam is concerned only with the bodies, not the souls of human beings, with literal not spiritual bread. By controlling the minds of men, Islam gains control over their bodies and it does this in order to create the "perfect" society. Human souls are left to languish in this prison of mental bars. Skeptical inquiry is dampened because Islam surrounds and impinges on all subjects, thus, freedom of thought is gradually extinguished in order for Islamic righteousness, defined purely as conformity to Islam, to prevail. Individual self-expression, self-realization and self-awareness are bound on every side.

True righteousness, on the other hand, righteousness that is not coerced, naturally results from loving one's neighbors, "as oneself" as the Judeo-Christian tradition teaches. Here, the emphasis is on the individual not the group, and the will of the individual to love God with all his heart and mind as prerequisite, makes the individual will, not a set of codes of conduct, the ultimate determining factor in what is considered to be righteous conduct. Furthermore, individual acceptance of divine love reorients the person as a "child of God" and thus he becomes obligated to love other men as his brothers in the spiritual sense. But always the onus is on the individual who is free to discover goodness, truth and beauty (God's will) for himself, even if it contradicts the teachings of the dominant religious authority of the day.

If the supreme relationship is between the individual and a living and dynamic Spirit, then sin may possibly be redefined as the deliberate rebellion against that divine inner leading, and may therefore be committed even by following religious authority, which might not be in accordance with God's will *for that individual at that time.* The entire focus of the concept of righteousness in the Western tradition is on the individual not the collective.

Transcendent value is not material, nor is it entirely a product of the mind and so cannot be encased within a set of codes, or lists of "thou shalt nots." This is a truth liberals routinely extol, but conservatives instinctively take shelter in tradition and authority, fearing that the loosening of religious codes will result in the death of religion and the dissolution of society. Nonetheless, goodness, truth and beauty are free to be discovered within each individual person. And this discovery holds the purpose and essence of life. True religion is not a material matter of certain works obtaining certain rewards. Indeed, the concept of individual communion with spirit effectively precludes the concept of doctrinal finality, no matter what the religious authorities of our own day may claim or seek to claim.

On the other hand, Islam denies individual spiritual communion in favor of communal doctrinal adherence. The Islamic doctrine has completely usurped the divine prerogative. Islam has effectively *replaced God*. Since for Muslims the only allowable method of finding God's will is obedience to Islam, for all intents and purposes, Islam is God.

At the root of Islam I suspect is a denial of the purpose of suffering as evidenced by the effort to make society into one smooth running machine, where no one grates against anyone else because "sin" has been outlawed. Piety is ensured by the police (religious police, thought police and otherwise) and stiff punishments are meted out in the event virtue, in the form of conformity, is not upheld. Persons are not allowed to suffer the natural consequences of their sins; adulteresses, blasphemers, and so forth are eliminated in order that the group should remain uncontaminated and also none the wiser for their experience. In the case of blasphemy (impure speech) and apostasy (impure thought) the individual must be permanently expunged; for purity of the group as evidenced in the thought, word, and deed of the individuals comprising the group must be upheld to ensure social cohesion.

Like a hive of bees, the group must be protected by the sacrifice of the individual. Islam is the queen for which all individuals sacrifice, indeed they sacrifice the essence of life itself, its joys and happiness, including the supreme satisfaction of knowing God and doing his will (discovering what is right for oneself). All of life instead becomes a sacrifice.

We should also remember thst the riverbed not the river. The form and tradition, ritual and doctrine of a religion, may hold and transmit the water of life, but they are not the water itself. Too many people mistake religion for the dogmatic tradition in which it is held. If Jonah couldn't have been literally swallowed by a whale, if the Red Sea couldn't have parted for Moses, because these events so described defy the known laws of physics, then modern man is tempted to disregard all religion as simply a mass of fable and superstition, to be dismissed as easily as throwing out the trash. But then, moderns are left with no outlet for their natural, inborn religious impulse and so religion soon reverts back to magic and charms as we see so prominently displayed in the "New Age" movement, or the religious impulse may continue to revert even further to fetishism and taboo as in Islam.

Opposing what Winston Churchill called, "Christianity's opposite creed," is proving altogether too much for many who wish to either hold on to the secularist view that "religion is irrelevant" or to buy into the new prevailing myth that "all religion is good" instead. It seems they are actually attempting to absolve themselves of the necessity of moral choice.

As the light of truth shines upon reality and defines the outlines of evil, it is inevitable that some should mistake the bearers of this truth as the source of their fear, the fear of the necessity for decision, and lash out at those defining the conflict as evil dividers of humanity. For as secularists and Muslims themselves learn the truth about Islam's bloody doctrine and history, they must each individually make a moral decision and this they wish to avoid at all costs. Many secularists mistakenly view division itself as evil and so they work to minimize differences with a smooth coat of interreligious "we are the world" sentimentality. In the absence of truth, there is no necessity for division; therefore, truth itself becomes the enemy and secularists and some religionists unwittingly become the emotional defenders of lies.

Western civilization, if it is to survive, must reach back into that stream of thought that springs still unpolluted by the confusion of modernity for its refreshment. We must reach back to the true source of our metaphysical dream; back to ancient Greek ethics and Judeo-Christian morality, back to those ages when man last thought deeply about the nature of the real and endeavored sincerely to adapt his life to that reality, rather than vainly attempting the opposite.

2
Predestination

It is to our advantage to deconstruct Islam using Western modes of thought and not to rely on the explanations of Islam given by those who have an interest in its viability. Take, for example, the two contradictory concepts vying for supremacy in these Qur'anic verses.

Qur'an 3:145 "No soul will ever die unless it is Allah's will. The length of each life is predetermined according to the Scriptures. Those who wish to receive their reward in this world will receive it, and those who wish to receive their reward in the world to come will also receive it. And We will undoubtedly reward those who serve Us with gratitude."

3:154 "Then, after the trouble Allah sent down upon you, He sent down calmness to wash over some of you. Some were overtaken by sleep, and others lay awake, stirred by their own passions, ignorantly thinking unjust thoughts about Allah. And they ask, "What do we gain by this affair?" Say: Truly the affair is entirely in Allah's hands. They hide in their hearts that which they do not want to tell you. They speak out saying, "If we had any say in this affair then none of us would have been killed here." Say: *If you had stayed at home, those of you who were destined to be killed would have died regardless.* This has taken place so that Allah might test your faith and see what is in your hearts. Allah knows the deepest secrets of every heart. Those of you who fled in cowardice on the day the two armies met in battle must have been tricked by Satan because of some evil you have done. But now Allah has forgiven you for Allah is forgiving and gracious."

The first concept expressed here is that of testing that involves a notion of some sort of free of will on the part of those being tested and the other is the concept of predestination which essentially nullifies the concept of free will. Allah is depicted as being in such complete control that Muhammad's decision (or was it his decision?) to engage in this battle had nothing to do with the deaths of his men. They simply would have died anyway because their deaths were predestined and no action or non-action on the part of a mere human being can change that predetermined fact. One's number is simply up, so to speak. All those men, dead upon the field of battle, would have died in their beds regardless, and at the very same hour; therefore Muhammad could not reasonably be blamed for their deaths.

With Islam it is important to understand that opposites such as the concepts of predestination and free will do not negate one another. As Bill Warner has pointed out,[1] both are considered equally true because the Qur'an is considered to be perfect and immutable – it is all true. And so there is a need to identify the overall trend. Imagine a river: on the surface are swirling eddies and if one measured the direction of the water there, one would get opposite and conflicting directions even though below the surface the overall movement of the water is in one direction only. So it is with Islam. When one seeks to identify the overall movement and direction of Islamic thought, there are many who will point to eddies on the surface as evidence for a contrary proposition. It is my contention that where there is conflict between the will of man and the will of Allah, the will of Allah always triumphs in Islamic philosophy because the power of Allah is thought of as absolute and undivided: he does not curtail or restrain his power in any way. In other words, Allah does not respect the free will of man, in fact, human free will is illusory at best.

By this logic, all three thousand people who lost their lives on September 11, 2001 as a result of jihad action would have died at that hour regardless. And furthermore, because Allah did not intervene, this is proof it was Allah's will that the attacks were successful. The jihadis who perpetrated this act, were only puppets on a stage, obeying the will of Allah according to a pre-written script. They did not cause all those deaths and all that destruction; rather, according to Islamic logic, Allah caused it as punishment for our sins, the sins of America as a collective entity.

---

1 Warner, Bill "The Dhimmi Revolution" *New English Review* (March 2007)

This further reduces to: everything that occurs in the reality of the material world is a direct result of Allah's will. Human will is but an instrument of the will of Allah and therefore does not have an independent existence in the overall trend of Islamic thought. Even though the concept of "testing" is present, Allah's will is never subservient to human will.

I contend this is the equivalent to asserting not that everything is God's will, but rather, that nothing is God's will, or even that there is no God, because there is no distinction between what is and what is not God's will in the reality of the material world: the good and the evil deeds of man are both equally and ultimately the result of the will of Allah. In the view of Islam, as Pope Benedict XVI pointed out in his Regensburg address, God's purpose is so transcendent as to be unknowable, which is to say, God is unknowable to the individual. And again there is no practical difference between that and the assertion that God does not exist, for His will, and therefore God himself, according to Islam, cannot be known. This is equivalent to saying that the difference between good and evil cannot be known, and this is so regardless of the existence of a list of accepted and prohibited actions put forth as "God's will" by Islam on the basis of Muhammad's example as the ultimate arbiter between truth and error. Goodness and truth do not have an independent existence; they are entirely dependent on the Islamic creed.

Furthermore, according to Winston Churchill, the Muslim belief in predestination engenders a "fearful, fatalistic apathy" which "paralyses the social development of those who follow it,"[2] for Allah's will is fixed in a one-size-fits-all pattern and is not unique to the individual believer. The individual's relationship to Allah is bound completely by the believer's obedience to Islam. Therefore, believers in Islam are actually barred from the greatest adventure known to man, that of finding God, meaning, goodness, truth and beauty, as an individual experiential reality. This is so because Allah's will is so transcendent as to be incomprehensible. Thus the "testing" of the believer is reduced to a test of conformity to the creed rather than a testing of the ability to discover what is right and true uniquely for himself. The most heinous acts, col-

---

2 Winston S. Churchill, *The River War*, first edition, Vol. II (Longmans, Green & Co., London 1899) pg. 248

lective and individual, can be rationalized as "Allah's will" and this of course is a prescription for social chaos. The violence and attitudes that the canonical texts of Islam naturally give rise to are repeatedly demonstrated wherever Islam is suddenly unconstrained, as witnessed after the American removal of Saddam Hussein's regime in Iraq.

According to Richard Weaver, the endowing of cultural forms with the idea of immanence historically gives rise to social cruelty. [3] It is the deification of a cultural system, such as the deification of the Church during the years of the Inquisition, or the deification of a political system such as communism, that creates conditions in which human sacrifice, often on a massive scale, becomes justified. In this view, the cultural structure essentially replaces the concept of a living God (dealing directly with autonomous human beings) and thus human freedom, happiness and ultimately lives are sacrificed to the cultural form in proportion to the fanaticism engendered by the belief in it. Thomas Mann writes,

> "And has not form two aspects? Is it not moral and immoral at once; moral insofar as it is the result of discipline, immoral – yes, actually hostile to morality – in that of its very essence it is indifferent to good and evil, and deliberately concerned to make the moral world stoop beneath its proud and undivided scepter?" [4]

Indeed, if morality is not conceived and actuated as being an individual matter, must it not at some point become coercive and cruel? And what could be conceived of as more cruel than the removal of an individual's God-given freedom? Under Islam, the removal of that freedom is so complete as to deny it exists at all.

Another bedrock problem lies in the failure of Islam to recognize God as a self-limited or self-limiting being, at least in so far as he acts within the material world of time and space (both obviously limiting factors separating the finite from the infinite). The existence of natural law is further evidence of this. Christianity recognizes a God who

---

3 See Weaver, Richard M., *Visions of Order* (Louisiana State University Press 1964, re-published by Intercollegiate Studies Institute 1995)
4 Mann, Thomas, *Death in Venice* (1912) as quoted in Weaver, *Visions of Order* pg. 73

is not whimsical, who has set his laws in motion and does not violate them. Thus, these laws may be discovered by the reasoning creature and therefore science, and all that flows from science, becomes possible because it is first conceivable.

Another limitation of God is the divine respect evidently given to human free will. Indeed, in the western world at least, if someone claims to be coerced by God, ("God made me do it") we consider that person to be of doubtful sanity. However, according to Islamic thought, Allah is not limited by natural law, or by reason, or even by goodness and truth. Said Pope Benedict XVI in his Regensburg address of Sept 12, 2006:

> "As opposed to this, the faith of the Church has always insisted that between God and us, between his eternal Creator Spirit and our created reason there exists a real analogy, in which unlikeness remains infinitely greater than likeness, yet not to the point of abolishing analogy and its language (cf. Lateran IV). God does not become more divine when we push him away from us in a sheer, impenetrable voluntarism; rather, the truly divine God is the God who has revealed himself as logos and, as logos, has acted and continues to act lovingly on our behalf. Certainly, love transcends knowledge and is thereby capable of perceiving more than thought alone (cf. Eph 3:19); nonetheless it continues to be love of the God who is logos. Consequently, Christian worship is worship in harmony with the eternal Word and with our reason (cf. Rom 12:1)."[5]

The unspoken assertion here is that the divine will can be known, that good and evil can be distinguished by reason, and that God can be approached through the mind – by our decisions first to know goodness and to then be good. In Islam, on the contrary, the bridge to God through the reasoning mind is cut. Allah demands unquestioning obedience and total sacrifice, including the sacrifice of the ability to distinguish good from evil as an individual, private matter. The will of Allah is not a personal experience. To reiterate, the Islamic system has totally

---

5 Quoted from *Catholic World News* online:
http://www.cwnews.com/news/viewstory.cfm?recnum=46474

usurped the place of the living God for the believer: worship and obedience are one.

I believe most Christians and Jews would concur: neither scripture, nor ritual, nor community, nor the religious edifice of the church or synagogue is God. They would also concur that God's will can be known as good and that good can be distinguished from evil by the human mind even without reliance on scripture or religious teaching. These things are guides which help the believer to find God in his own soul. But when religious forms, in their arrogance, become a substitute for God, then the potential for evil and the cruelty of cultural coercion rapidly ensue.

In order for cultural progress to occur, man must be free to distinguish the greater from the lesser. For example, which is the greater evil: adultery itself, or stoning as punishment? Jews and Christians answered long ago: the stoning is the greater evil. Muslims, on the contrary, and despite their modern protestations that "this is not the true Islam," are forever barred from making such a judgment, because the will of Allah is absolutely transcendent and unreachable through the human mind.

Therefore, what western reason would deem psychopathological murder/suicide, Islam calls the "martyrdom of the sainted" and does so without guile because the reason of Islam exists entirely within the bounds of Islam. A bridge of reason simply does not exist between our two worlds, as it does not exist between the individual Muslim and the will of Allah.

Reason cannot compromise with unreason without destroying the basis for its existence. By the same token, unreason cannot become reasonable without destroying itself as well. There is simply no way the hoped-for "reform" of Islam by way of reason would not end in Islam's ultimate destruction, but this is not an outcome to be feared. It should be welcomed.

Beginning in the 19th Century, reason has been vigorously applied to the investigation of Jewish and Christian scripture in the form of higher criticism. Much of modern day biblical scholarship is concerned with separating historical truth from the product of what may be charitably called "enthusiastic editing," that is, the probable embellishments to Jewish history that often involve the miraculous intervention of God. For example, biblical scholars are concerned with how much of the Exodus story is actual history and how much might be fanciful. Is Moses a real historic figure or a creation of the human imagination? Did the Jews flee Egypt en masse as recited in Exodus? Are there any independent historical records that can verify the biblical account? Are there any archeological records that could provide some kind of independent verification? In other words, Western historians want to know whether the Exodus story is true in its entirety, or if some of it is true (and if so, which parts?), or if none of it is true.

To begin with, this presupposes that truth can actually be known, or at least increasingly approximated, and furthermore that the truth is important to know. In other words, there is a common thirst for truth that drives Western man toward the ever greater discovery of truth – truth in more detail, truth in more depth and breadth, truth as separate and distinct from error and falsehood. In the West, truth is revered because it is equated with reality and furthermore we allow there is only one reality to know. We may concede that all human truths are relative, but we share the common belief that the truth of any matter may be increasingly approximated by the use of unitary reason. Something is either real or it isn't and if we have before us two contradictory statements or accounts, then we know that at least one of them is false.

In Islamic thought a different standard applies, if anything contradicts Islamic doctrine it is considered to be false and as Bill Warner points out, Islam is a duel system of thought which holds that two contradictory facts can *both* be true.[6] There is no one truth or one reality to discover or to separate from unreality. The proposition that two contradictory facts can both be true destroys the value of truth and indeed the entire western concept of Truth. In Western philosophy there is only one Truth. In Islam, truth is duel and is neither sacred nor revered. One might postulate that reason itself would be destroyed by such a system, but that is not the case. Islam is a system that flows logically from its premises.

It is useful to remember at this point that there is a difference between what *has* value and what *is* value – or is something by which value is measured. Truth is a value and we evaluate reality in accordance

6 Warner, Bill "The Dhimmi Revolution" *New English Review* (March 2007)

with how much truth is contained in our understanding of it. Asking if something is true is essentially the same as asking if it is real. We posit that reality can be known because the truth about reality can be ascertained (or approximated) and this relative truth may be discerned from falsehood using our rules of reason. Traditionally for the western world, truth exists and it exists independently and transcendently as an absolute value. It is a yardstick by which reality is measured.

In Islam, the relation between truth and reality is severed. Truth is not extolled, but rather enslaved to expediency, specifically to the advance of Islam. Therefore, there has been no attempt by Muslims to independently verify any of the stories in the Koran and no attempt to separate the historical Muhammad from the "enthusiastic editing" by some handlers of the Qur'an, Hadiths and Sira, though this probability seems quite self-evident to the casual Western reader. This train of thought is not even allowed to Muslims who, if they are pious, must simply believe unquestioningly in the divine and uncreated nature of the Qur'an and in the prophethood of Muhammad.

Muhammad claimed to be a prophet, specifically the last prophet, in the Hebrew line of prophets. This explains the attempt in the Qur'an to assert that his lineage traced back to Abraham, through his son Ismail, and that Islam is another, indeed the one true, branch of Judaism.

The Qur'an purports to be "revealed" history with the effect that Muslims must believe in that history without any independent verification. For example, Muslims believe Abraham built the Kaaba (in which the black fetish stone mentioned earlier is housed) and would never think to seek after secondary sources either archaeologically or from ancient records in the way Western biblical scholars naturally would. There are no historic records existing before the Qur'an to indicate Abraham made the long journey from Hebron to Mecca.

Indeed, the Higher Criticism of the nineteenth century, that is the work of biblical scholars that begins in the time of Julius Wellhausen and continues today, with Jaroslav Pelikan to find out more about the "historical Jesus" or about the truth, or fiction, of what is contained in both the Old and the New Testaments, even going so far as to use carbon-dating techniques on tombs in the Holy Land – has no analogue when it comes to Islam. For Muslims, there can be no questioning of the existence of Muhammad and the details of his life, as they were fixed early on, and even the discussion of how in the first few centuries of Islam the "Islamic narrative" had not been completely fixed, or the fact that there is more than one "version" of the Qur'an in existence (they differ very slightly, but they do differ)[7] is deeply discouraged.

Raphael Patai describes the essential Islamic attitude as a "disregard for reality and inclination to adhere to ideal constructs," which puts it very well. He goes on to say:

> "It may be mentioned in passing that Arabic historical writing very frequently took the form of biographies of people of a particular type and that Arabic histories are often replete with anachronisms and confused in detail and chronology. This lack of concern with historical sequence and dates is apparent in the *tarikh* (History) of the famous traditionalist al-Bukari (810-870). This work contains biographies of the men whose names appear in isnads, or authorities for traditions going back to Muhammad: but, less than 7 per cent of the biographies are provided with dates of death, less than one-half of one percent of them give an indication of the date of birth, and only a little more than one-half of one per cent contain, in addition, some date which fixes the time of their subject." [8]

For the Western mind, the importance of fixing dates in the *isnad* chain goes without saying. The absence of dates effectively renders the chain worthless for Westerners and yet for Muslims fixing the date of when something happened is almost completely disregarded. And like ancient Hebrew, the Arabic language has no clear past and future verb tenses, but while Modern Hebrew has modified these tenses to be more in line with other modern languages, Arabic has not. Classical Arabic has been made sacred by Islam and so is considered perfect. Like Islam itself, it is not to be changed nor is it to be subject to implied criticism through, for example, attention being paid to problems such

---

7 See Ibn Warraq, "Which Koran?" Parts I and II in *New English Review* (Feb.-March 2008)

8 Patai, Raphael, *The Arab Mind* (Charles Scribner's Sons, New York, revised ed. 1983) pg. 71

as the absence of clear verb tenses.

The language problem may have been one reason why Jesus and Moses are mistakenly cast as contemporaries in the Qur'an. The past is just a story, reality is irrelevant. History, as we understand it in the West, is not contained in the Qur'an and traditional Qur'anic history itself is now thought to be almost entirely fabricated.[9] The Qur'an is a replacement for history, outside of and superior to mundane historical facts. The Muslim attitude is that nothing that occurred before the coming of the Qur'an is of any consequence. History begins with Muhammad. All previous records are considered worthless (as stemming from the *Time of Ignorance* or *jahiliyya*) and are replaced by the Qur'anic version. This has consequences: peoples who have been Islamized are discouraged from taking any interest in, or even preserving the artifacts of, their own pre-Islamic past. The ruin visited upon the Bamiyan Buddhas was simply the latest example of the vast destruction that Muslims have inflicted, not only on the monuments and statuary important to faiths that preceded Islam, but also to all non-Islamic, and therefore essentially worthless, works.

The Old Testament, on the other hand, is a collection of the writing of various authors recording the history of the Hebrew people over the centuries. Everyone understands that some of the oldest writings were written from the perspective of a much more primitive conception of God and the universe, but these are generally understood as examples of the thoughts and ideas of an ancient and more barbaric time. The Old Testament also contains some of the loftiest and most noble thoughts about God in all recorded history. And while some of the Bible is clearly inspired, some of it is definitely not inspired, and it is certainly the case most thinking people in the West do not regard the Bible as having been directly dictated by God in the same way the way the Qur'an is regarded by most Muslims. The Bible is not strictly history, nor is it entirely myth and fable, but combines elements of both.

Islam has overthrown truth with its substitution of duality and so has no real grasp on reality. Islam engenders confusion and encourages what Hugh Fitzgerald calls "the habit of mental submission" which stifles curiosity. Knowledge for its own sake is alien. Everything is eval-

---

9 Ibn Warraq, "A Conference On The Early History Of Islam And The Koran" *New English Review* (May 2008)

uated on one criterion: does it advance Islam or not? Even time itself is not regarded as especially important or perhaps not even as necessarily real, but rather as part of the fabric of predestination in which all things, (including the good men do as well as the evil they do) are the direct result of God's will, not of their own. A man's destiny and even his character are thought to be unchangeable. So even given the desire of Muslims to change something in their character or behavior, there is no use in trying to change, or to attempt to grow in the spirit due to the fact that they regard their lives as predestined and unchangeable regardless. Inshallah is the telling everyday phrase, but behind that phrase is an entire mental universe, in which a whimsical Allah decides everything and his decisions are not to be questioned or subject to appeal: Allah ta'allah. Allah Knows Best. That is why one finds among Muslims little discernible moral striving, only the striving to follow the rules of Islam as closely and minutely as possible. Morality, as we understand it, is irrelevant. As Andre Servier notes:

> "Islam is a doctrine of death, inasmuch as the spiritual not being separated from the temporal, and every manifestation of activity being subjected to dogmatic law, it formally forbids any change, any evolution, any progress. It condemns all believers to live, to think, and to act as lived, thought and acted the Musulmans of the second century of the Hegira [8th century A.D.], when the law of Islam and its interpretation were definitely fixed.
>
> "After a century of Arab domination, there is a complete annihilation of all intellectual culture." [10]

This is not hard to understand, for once Truth is abandoned, knowledge too becomes ultimately meaningless and the individual ability to distinguish truth from error, to participate in the progressive discovery of reality, is not allowed. Truth and morality are what Islam says they are, no more, no less. And so, having been denied independent judgment, the Muslim mind becomes fully enslaved to the

10 Servier, Andre, *Islam and the Psychology of the Musulman*, (Translated by A. S. Moss-Blundell, Scribner's New York, 1924)

mental complexities and physical intricacies of Islam. The result being that, under Islam, the life of the mind is deliberately stifled. It is only the "bad" Muslim, the Muslim who begins to question, even if he must publicly refrain from much questioning, who exhibits the kind of mental activity that we in the West, outside of such totalitarian interludes as the Nazis and the Communists, now take for granted and, indeed, wish to encourage. To quote Gustave von Grunebaum,

> "It is essential to realize that Muslim civilization is a cultural entity that does not share our primary aspirations. It is not vitally interested in analytical self-understanding, and it is even less interested in the structural study of other cultures, either as an end in itself or as a means toward clearer understanding of its own character and history. If this observation were to be valid merely for contemporary Islam, one might be inclined to connect it with the profoundly disturbed state of Islam, which does not permit it to look beyond itself unless forced to do so. But as it is valid for the past as well, one may perhaps seek to connect it with the basic antihumanism of this civilization, that is, the determined refusal to accept man to any extent whatever as the arbiter or the measure of things, and the tendency to be satisfied with truth as description of mental structures, or in other words, with psychological truth.

> "The absolute is self-contained; absolute truth is self-sufficient; the study of error and imperfection for their own sake does not deserve a supreme collective effort. The non-Muslim world is interesting enough, but, in a sense, obsolete, its foundations outmoded ever since the final revelation manifested through the Prophet the changeless norms of individual behavior and social structure, and the grace of God allowed them to be implemented (within limits, it is true) in the Muslim community.

> "This attitude leads to an extreme concern with power and success in history, or, more precisely, with success in history as the validation of revelation - an outlook that represents the sharp-

est possible contrast with the outlook that governs Christianity's encounter with history."[11]

Islam's sacralization of the profane and mundane, its failure to separate the material from the spiritual coupled with its failure to recognize progressive levels of morality and spiritual attainment, will forever condemn Muslims to lives of mental confusion and moral stagnation, while condemning their societies to barbarism.

The Western world is now rapidly acquainting itself with Islam, but it is highly unlikely that the Islamic world will reciprocate and acquaint itself with either Christian teaching or Jewish history. Islam is a closed system of self-imposed isolation. Short of the miraculous appearance of a new Muslim prophet, whose existence would be immediately extinguished by those ever faithful to the "Last Seal of the Prophets," there is little hope for changing Islam, or the mental habits it inculcates.

And though we may pray for miracles, we should prepare the strategies of war so to protect our civilization from destruction, even knowing that it may not be possible. We must confirm truth exists by living lives loyal to the idea that there are truths, that the very idea of Truth is an important one, and though we may never arrive at it, it is the journey – the attainment of some asymptotic approximation of those truths or that Truth that matters.

---

11 von Grunebaum, Gustave, *Modern Islam: The Search for Cultural Identity* (Greenwood Press, Westport Ct., 1962) pp. 55-58

3

Piety and Wonder

In her book, *The Force of Reason*, Oriana Fallaci makes the striking argument that war is an integral part of the natural world; even that war is inherent in the struggle for existence. Says she:

> "War is not a curse which characterizes human nature: it is a curse which characterizes Life. There is no way to avoid war because war is a part of Life. Repulsive, hideous? Of course. So hideous that my atheism stems mainly from it. That is, from my refusal to accept the idea of a Creator who invented a world where Life kills Life, where Life eats Life. A world where in order to survive one has to kill and eat other living beings. Be they chickens or clams or tomatoes. If such an existence had been conceived by a Creator, I say, that Creator would be a very nasty one indeed." [1]

I believe this to be the feeling of a great many people today; people who are at least two generations removed from the soil and who no longer work with nature and thus feel independent of her, disconnected from her, and are now turning scornful and resentful of the natural world. Many people today are no longer in awe of the mystery of existence, but are judgmental of it; and instead of feeling gratitude for the privilege of being, are more likely to feel resentful toward the decay of the physical form. Fallaci rages "against the dying of the light," against life itself, and her anguish is of course understandable to anyone who has ever suffered.

Carried within this attitude is also the modern posture of science and technology with their combined and continuing aggressive assault upon nature. Modern man is given to understand that nature may be transcended through technology. If the climate is too hot, we

1 Fallaci, Oriana, *The Force of Reason* (Rizzoli International, New York, 2006) pgs. 22-23

have air conditioning; too cold, we have central heat. Don't like your nose? We can change it. Don't like your sex? We can change that too. Don't like growing older? We can make you look younger. And so on. Nature is something to be feared and fought. Nature is viruses and bacteria. Nature is hurricanes and tornadoes and earthquakes. Nature is illness. Nature is decay. Nature is death. Commenting on this state of affairs, Richard Weaver wrote:

> "I would maintain that modern man is a parricide. He has taken up arms against, and he has effectively slain, what former men have regarded with filial veneration. He has not been conscious of crime but has, on the contrary – and certainly this is nothing new to students of human behavior – regarded his action as a proof of virtue.

> "It is highly significant to learn that when Plato undertakes a discussion of the nature of piety and impiety, he chooses as interlocutor a young man who is actually bent upon parricide. Eurthyphro, a youth filled with arrogant knowledge and certain he understands "what is dear to the gods," has come to Athens to prosecute his father for murder. Struck by the originality of this proceeding, Socrates questions him in the usual fashion. His conclusion is that piety, which consists of co-operation with the gods in the kind of order they have instituted, is a part of the larger concept of justice. It can be added that the outcome of the dialectic does not encourage the prosecution. The implication is that Euthyphro has no right, out of his partial and immature knowledge, to proceed contemptuously against an ancient relationship.

> "In our contemporary setting the young man stands for science and technology, and the father for the order of nature. For centuries now we have been told that our happiness requires an unrelenting assault upon this order; dominion, conquest, triumph – all these names have been used as if it were a military campaign. Somehow the notion has been loosed that nature is hostile to man or that her ways are offensive or slovenly, so that

every step of progress is measured by how far we have altered these. Nothing short of recovery of the ancient virtue of *pietas* can absolve man from this sin." [2]

At the other extreme are environmentalists who view nature as a form of divine perfection which has been corrupted by the machinations of ugly mankind. These people seem to come very close to nature worship. Indeed, with the modern breakdown of metaphysical reasoning, 21st century man seems in many ways to have reverted to his ancient religious posture embodied in the fear and worship of nature. With no metaphysic to give him distance and perspective on the natural world, modern man lurches between two extremes: nature must be venerated and protected on the one hand, or conquered and exploited on the other, there is no middle ground.

Intelligent Design in one sense is a reaction to this loss of piety toward nature. Modern science gives man the mistaken impression that nature has no mysteries remaining to her and that all natural phenomena may be explained as a simple chain reaction of cause and effect, with need neither to reference a first cause nor to consider a final effect. The bridge to the next level of intellectual integration, the meaning of life in other words, has been burned. And if life itself has no meaning, then the obvious conclusion for the layman is that *his* life has no meaning either. Indeed, if life contains no meaning, neither can it contain any purpose. So by pointing to all that is unknown, the Intelligent Design movement, for all its faults, is attempting to restore our sense of wonder and humility toward nature, even a sense of piety and reverence, which has been forgotten in the rush of scientific conquest; but which is the proper posture of man toward nature.

Human beings consistently seek affirmation of their existence and a sense of belonging. Of particular poignancy is the modern reverence for mass communication embodied in the desire to be on television, for there is a semblance of meaning in fame. Those whose faces are recognizable to large numbers of people through this medium seem to be perceived as *more real* because their reality exists in a larger realm, in a larger community: their reality is shared and thus they touch a certain

2 Weaver, Richard, *Ideas Have Consequences* (University of Chicago Press, 1948) pgs. 170-171

oneness, but oneness not with God, in the sense of higher values or higher truths; but with man, and so immediately values are lowered.

One truly wonders if murderers are doing their evil work in an ever more heinous fashion in order to gain that mystical communion with their fellows through the television screen. That they are known is more important than what they are known for. The person is more important than the virtue, man is elevated above God, and the world is turned upside down.

Particularly pathetic are the poor souls playing to the crowd and parading every vice known to man on television shows like the one hosted by Jerry Springer; humiliating themselves and their families before the world in order to "be on TV," because being on TV seems to be the only thing in the modern world containing the power to make someone a person of significance. You are somebody if your face is on television. The cry of the masses is: "I want to be real!" And this is the only way that looks promising to them, for religion, true religion, in the sense man used to have of identifying with spiritual value or moral truth as a way of "becoming real," has vanished. The conscious development of righteousness of character along with a sense of spiritual progress is so eroded a concept as to be almost imperceptible in modern life. Substituted is a proliferation of literature consisting of various guides to self-affirmation; but we cannot affirm ourselves to ourselves and come away with anything of value. The masses watching Jerry Springer know they must seek affirmation from outside themselves, and since they cannot seek it from a God they are told does not exist, they seek it from a mystical union with man, which is worship of man.

Islam crystallizes the worship of man both in the concept of the ummah, or "community of believers" which takes absolute precedence over the individual, and also in the worshipful veneration of one specific man, Muhammad, so much so, that the tiniest details of his personal habits are imitated to this day. His likes and dislikes along with the sayings and doings of Muhammad form the entire basis for good and evil in the Islamic system. There is no other measure. In Islam, man (in abstract) is not the measure of all things; one specific man is. Islam puts man in place of God, the material in place of the spiritual, and the group in place of the individual; and for certain we see its fruits.

But let us consider nature. If we look carefully at the natural world one of the first things we notice is the great individuality expressed there. No two blossoms, butterfly wings, blades of grass or snowflakes are exactly alike. And when we look at butterfly wings, for example, we grasp plainly a geometric pattern and we also grasp, just as plainly, that what makes the wing a particular individual wing, is its deviation from that perfect pattern, as it exists in the abstract. The same with blossoms, each one varies in a color and pattern.

At the same time we witness in living things a seeking after an ever more perfect expression. Plants, for example, are constantly moving and jockeying for a more perfect position in relation to light above and water beneath. There seems to be inherent in life a yearning, not simply to *be*, but to *become*, and to become more "perfect" even though this perfection exists only as an abstraction "in the mind of God." For example, a rose expresses "roseness" in the sense of complying with a pre-existent perfect form and simultaneously expresses that roseness in a unique and individual fashion.

There can be no concept of spiritual progress without the concept of "perfecting" one's life individually, of substituting higher motives in place of baser ones, of adapting oneself to a universe containing moral law. Every businessman knows that "what goes around, comes around" and the successful ones find lasting success by dealing honestly and fairly with both customers and creditors. The concept of karma has been borrowed for modern usage to express this concept of an objective, morally structured, universe that must be dealt with on its own terms. Our fathers took for granted that "God is not mocked," but modern man is no longer certain of this. If God doesn't exist, then how can there be sin? How can we proclaim a better way to live when so many proudly profit from living lives dominated by greed and lust, and do so without shame?

Pride and sloth are currently celebrated, as is the casual feeding of the sexual appetite. Consequently, crime escalates and broken homes proliferate. Man is no longer responsible for the care of an immortal soul, so we no longer seek to secure our eternal destiny through the gradual perfecting of that soul; rather we are reduced to pursuing of the perfect orgasm instead.

What we think of as culture often consists of an insistence on self-control. It is that conformity which delivers man from the slavery of his passions. It reminds man he is not the center of the universe and that self-indulgence is the prelude to self-destruction. Now, having abandoned the concept of God's will, or morality, as an objective reality, we are left with no "should be," no basis for righteousness, indeed no basis for right versus wrong at all. Thus our culture has become directionless with no way of judging better or worse outside individual egotistical desire and we see the wreckage this has caused all around us. There can be no doubt, we live in a disintegrating culture. We have lost our metaphysical dream.

Modern man is taught that he is naturally good and that evil, if it exists at all, originates from forces outside the self or, specifically in the case of Islam, outside the group. Modern man is taught there is no higher will than his own, so, if he owes responsibility to anything, it is to his fellows, the community. The communal good is the highest good. Communal loyalty, extended to embrace all humanity, is the highest form of devotion, and the advance of an earthly kingdom is substituted for the advance of the heavenly one in the hearts of men. Islam, as an extreme form of this thought, engenders no sense of wonder toward that which is "outside," for it recognizes no greater reality than the Islamic system itself.

To recover true piety, it is first necessary to recover our sense of wonder toward a reality greater than ourselves and much greater than any human system of thought, a reality that is infinitely complex and infinitely beautiful, with layer upon layer of meaning and ultimately of value as well. We must eventually come to recognize that goodness, truth, and beauty exist as realities outside ourselves, realities that existed before we were born and will continue to exist after we are gone from this world. We may even contemplate them as existing eternally in order to recover the metaphysical dream that once integrated Western thought.

Perhaps it is necessary to discover love as a reality in the inner world before we can see it as a reality in the outer world, but once it is truly discovered, the former world of war, struggle, ugliness and death, gradually transforms into a world of fantastic beauty and awe-inspiring complexity. Indeed we may conclude that the universe we inhabit is a good and benevolent place and that love is the very substance of life.

In the absence of this spiritual orientation, once an integral part of Western thought, modern man lurches between "sentimentality on the one hand and brutality on the other"[3] with no middle ground in between. We are supposed to be able to find meaning in our individual lives but we are not allowed to integrate that meaning into a larger framework; so we live with a central contradiction (meaning vs. non-meaning) that allows us to tolerate a myriad of other contradictions, and finally we are left with no reliable way to distinguish levels of value.

The human mind, which was once thought of as the great arena of moral decision-making, filled with tragedy and pathos and consequences eternal, is now thought to simply be a repository of sensory input. The former majesty and grandeur of human life is reduced to the process of filling up the data bank, which is of course promptly destroyed upon physical death, leaving nothing behind but the faulty and temporary records in the data banks of others, or the scribbling on paper, which will also be destroyed in the end. Is it any wonder the masses flock to entertainment and seek self-indulgence as a means of staving off these conclusions?

And is it any wonder the worship of man and materialism in the form of Islam has come to claim adherents? And is it not the purpose of this materialistic creed to deny the reality and substance of love? Witness Muslim brothers beating and killing their sisters. Muslim fathers murdering their own daughters. Everyone sacrificing their sons and brothers to jihad. An inner "thought police" so powerful as to never allow deviation from the thought system, a system that must deny the existence of that which it cannot control, a system at war with human affection. But who can deny this is the direction our materialistic culture is tending?

In order to remedy this state of affairs we must begin by admitting the reality of the unseen substance of life. Like the wind, we do not behold it directly, but we perceive it in its effects upon the material world; living matter is qualitatively different from dead matter. Second, we must restore the concept of God's will as the highest good, or of good as a transcendent value, and redefine sin as deliberate rebellion against this Good. Third, we must come to acknowledge that it is not

3 Weaver, Richard, *Ideas Have Consequences* (University of Chicago Press, 1948) pg. 22

necessary to grasp a concept in its entirety, but it is necessary to grasp the concept of the existence of higher concepts. In other words, we needn't grasp truth absolutely in order to grasp the concept of the necessary existence of absolute Truth. Fourth, we must begin to approach our own existence with some degree of humility, recognizing that the order of the universe contains mysteries we cannot fathom and complexities we will never fully understand. And when we look out upon the stars we ought to be awed by the vastness of creation and when we look upon a microscopic cell we ought to be awed by its intense complexity and intricate beauty. We may even allow this feeling of awe to cultivate within us a sense of proper piety toward Nature.

Unfortunately, our entire culture has been involved in indicting Nature and the God of nature as immoral for centuries. Our highest understanding of God as Love is degraded not only by modern Darwinian scientism, but also by millennia old concepts concerning the nature of God as wrathful, vengeful and angry, which is the very picture of God Islam embraces, and so we are lost in a jumble of confusion. If God is a mixture of good and evil, if He directs evil toward man as in the book of Job, then how can we love, venerate or worship him? How can we trust and have faith in him? Indeed, how is it possible to avoid placing him on trial by way of human judgment? For if God is not unified goodness, how can we *not* place ourselves and our moral sensibility above his? And indeed, are not all totalitarianisms based, at bottom, on the concept that man is morally superior to God and that the reality God created is unjust and corrupt?

The indictment of the West by Islam is very much based on the notion that man should not put himself above God. But of course, by constructing "God's law" directly from the life of a man, and a man with more than a few, shall we say, character flaws at that, Muslims are in fact guilty of the crime of which they accuse the West: placing man, indeed, one man (Muhammad frozen is aspic), above God. Furthermore, Islam firmly clings to the olden anthropomorphic notion of God's character as bloodthirsty and warlike, presernted as a revival of religious authenticity. The modern Judeo-Christian world must make an equally firm stand for God's character as loving and fatherly, for these core conceptions determine the nature of the societies we inhabit. But to do this, Christians must examine Christianity itself and separate the gospel of

Jesus from the engulfing bed of twenty centuries of theological layering which created the theological schisms that spawned anti-Semitism and the numerous internecine Christian wars.

Even though the West lost sight of God as a personal being during the Enlightenment, it kept hold of goodness as a concept of absolute value for a time, but this conception has weakened considerably along with the increasing mechanization of society. It seems the closer man lives to the soil, the more likely he is to view nature, and by extension God, as good. The further he is removed from the soil, the more likely he is to view the natural world with suspicion, even fear and contempt. Today, a child's view of nature is likely to be formed by watching sensational gore-filled nature programs as shown on television and he is constantly exhorted to fear germs and disease. The message thereby instilled in young minds is this: Nature is evil. The world is an evil place. Goodness does not exist and therefore, God does not exist.

If our culture is to regenerate, and regenerate it must in order to face down Islam over the long haul, then certain core cultural concepts must be revived, and first among these is the concept of goodness. Goodness is pure value, nothing else. It is not time or space dependent. It stands above reason and gives reason order. Goodness may also be viewed as a final level of intellectual integration or as a primary organizing concept. Moving downward from goodness flows mercy and from mercy flows justice and from justice flows honor and from honor flows duty. Thus, if the concept of goodness is lost, all that flows from it likewise becomes meaningless. Without a firm grasp on the transcendent, man is thrown back upon himself, a victim of directionless scientific dialectic, without purpose, without meaning. And as we have seen, with nothing beyond himself to live for or to strive for, man becomes a pitiable creature vainly endeavoring to elevate his lusts to some level of profundity.

Man, it seems, is dropped into this world as a questioning stranger born in tension, fear and doubt. No other creature struggles over the purpose of life, no other creature experiences moral conflict. Significantly, no other creature but man bears the gift of language or can express its will with all the subtlety language provides. Each human utterance, each thought, is an expression of *will*. Thus man seems to be provided with freedom of will above and beyond that of any other living creature, and is endowed with a moral sense and the ability to recognize value other creatures show no sign of possessing.

Our cultural imagination has always striven to deliver man from himself and to elevate him above the base animal level of existence (money and sex). When examined, our culture is found to be based upon such concepts such as justice, honor and duty and thus society becomes utterly lost and adrift once its tether to transcendent goodness is cut.

On the other hand, according to Islamic doctrine, God (Allah) is most expressly *not* good, and thus the lesser organizing concepts, mercy, justice, honor and duty, to continue our example, are perverted to their opposite meanings. It is crucial we recognize this fact, for each culture is using the same words, but with opposite meanings, and this is creating great confusion especially among those eager to see good (and thus harmlessness) in Islam.

The question then is, in modern industrial society, can the concept of goodness survive minus an intrinsic identification between the concept of the absolute, infinite and eternal good and thus with God? In other words, if goodness is reduced to a mere relativity, can it remain good?

In modern Christian doctrine, there is a great stumbling block to the recovery of this concept of God as good, and that is the atonement doctrine. According to this train of theological thought, God required the sacrifice of his sinless son in order to propitiate his wrath against fallen mankind. It was only through this, the penultimate sacrifice, that total redemption from sin was thought to have been made possible. Jesus took on the sins of the world, was sacrificed, and thus became the path of redemption. His exemplary teachings were thereby reduced to an adjunct to the centrality of his sacrifice.

But is this the vision of God Jesus himself brought to the world? Did Jesus not repeatedly emphasize the loving nature of God and man's redemption through faith alone? Was the life of Jesus not a lens through which man might glimpse the nature of God? And if so, do we see through Christ a God of wrath and vengeance? If not, might there not some other interpretation of the Passion to be made? Must we be satisfied with such a schizophrenic and obviously primitive view of God?

Sin, obviously, did not end with the passion of Christ. The "long, lamentable catalogue of human crime" continues to find new additions unabated throughout the course of our history. It is a very powerful and especially emotional idea to feel that our sins somehow retroactively cause the suffering of Christ, the suffering of God. But perhaps we are missing something else.

Central to all faith is the concept of the will of God and central to the atonement doctrine is the concept that the Father willed the death of the Son. In other words, the will of man is subordinate to the will of God. As we have seen, this idea is central to Islamic doctrine as well. And though this conception may be emotionally satisfying, it may also be a method of mere justification, since everything that occurs may be put down as "God's will," leading directly to religious fatalism, the opiate of the masses. So does God really negate the will of man? Or might the life of Jesus illustrate exactly how far the will of God is in reality subordinate to the will of man, at least during man's time on earth?

If all things come about through the will of God, then we must conclude that God wills evil, which is exactly the simplistic conclusion of Islam. But if we take a broader view, and see God as allowing human will to indulge in both good and evil, the life of Jesus, as God and man, becomes immediately more complex. Christians may view the figure of Jesus as the embodiment of goodness and personification of truth. As man, he portrayed the perfect submission to the Father's will, and as God, he portrayed the reality of *God's submission to the will of man,* for he allowed his own execution.

In this view, free will is God's gift to man and the endowment of language gives us an additional level of mental freedom, enhanced imagination. We are free to love God and to respond to his love, but we are also free to reject him, even to hate him and to formulate our reasons for doing so by way of our language endowment. According to this line of thought, the Father does not coerce the love of his children.

As we have seen, in Islam, human love of God is always subordinate to human obedience to Allah and thus obedience is unapologetically coerced. Free will, according to Islam, simply does not exist; rather everything that occurs in time is predestined as God's will.

"Freedom" is thought to only be found in complete subordination of the individual will to the Islamic system, thought to be "God's plan." This is slavery of the most cruel and barbaric kind, slavery of the mind and spirit. The western mind inherently rebels at the thought God would do such a thing to his children, we are revolted by this portrait of an un-loving God.

The Christian "Lord's Prayer" illustrates our understanding of free will perfectly: "thy kingdom come, thy will be done on earth as it is in heaven." Implied here is the understanding that God's will is not always done by his children. Perhaps those children were not carrying out God's will when they humiliated, scourged and crucified the innocent Jesus, but perhaps, and maybe more than just perhaps, Jesus carried out God's will when he voluntarily submitted himself to the natural outworking of human error and human passion, just they way he does every day and every hour. For having granted man his freedom, he would not arbitrarily rescind it, even at the cost of his human life. In this view, God is unified and consistent. On the existence of evil in the world, Jesus had this to say:

> "The kingdom of heaven is likened unto a man who sowed good seed in his field. But while the man slept, his enemy came and sowed tares among the wheat, and went his way. But when the blade was sprung up, and brought forth fruit, then appeared the tares also. So the servants of the householder came and said unto him, Sir, didst not thou sow good seed in thy field? From whence then hath it tares? He said unto them, An enemy hath done this. The servants said unto him, Wilt thou then that we go and gather them up? But he said, Nay; lest while ye gather up the tares, ye root up also the wheat with them. Let both grow together until the harvest: and in the time of harvest I will say to the reapers, Gather ye together first the tares, and bind them in bundles to burn them: but gather the wheat into my barn." [4]

In this parable, two things are clear. 1) God does not create evil, though he does allow it and 2) evil is a temporary phenomenon. This is

4 The Bible, Matthew 13:24-30, New International version

entirely consistent with the much, much older foundational document of Judeo-Christian thought put forth in Genesis: *"In the beginning God created the heaven and the earth... And God saw every thing that he had made, and, behold, it was very good."*

Perhaps the evil with which modern man attempts to indict God is in reality that of his own creation. Old, anthropomorphic concepts of God in which God is a source of evil, or that he is angry or vengeful or filled with wrath requiring appeasement through the sacrifice and suffering of the innocent are ancient concepts entirely unworthy to be included in modern theological thought. Perhaps the atonement doctrine will eventually be abandoned so that Christianity might recapture a greater truth in and through the life of Jesus. The religion revealed by Jesus during his life should eventually triumph over the religion that was developed by theologians about Jesus, which has concentrated largely, and in some sense almost exclusively, on the fact of his death. In this way can we revive the concept of good as a transcendental reality and of God as the personification of the ultimate, eternal and infinite Good.

4
Freedom True and False

Why do they hate us? ... They hate our freedoms – our freedom of religion, our freedom of speech, our freedom to vote and assemble and disagree with each other. – President George W. Bush, Sept. 21, 2001

Freedom is a word invoked constantly in America as a descriptive term for self-government and the concept of sovereignty of the people. The word itself conjures pride and patriotism and is an integral part of our national myth. It involves the idea of unlocking human potential, of opportunity, individualism and self-reliance. Freedom and the American ideal of individual self-realization are one and the same in the minds of most Americans. Freedom is that intangible thing we defend when we fight.

Less understood is the fact that the mujahadeen are also fighting for freedom, but a freedom very differently defined. According to the Muslim philosopher Sayyid Qutb,

> "This *din* [religion] is a universal declaration of the freedom of man from slavery to other men and to his own desires, which is also a form of human servitude. It is a declaration that the sovereignty belongs only to Allah, the Lord of all the worlds. It challenges all such systems based on the sovereignty of man, i.e., where man attempts to usurp the attribute of Divine sovereignty. Any system in which final decisions are referred to human beings, and in which the source of all authority are men, *deifies human beings* by designating others than Allah as lords over men." [1]

In Islamic terms, the western concept of political sovereignty

---

1 Qutb, Sayyid, *Milestones* (American Trust Publications, Indianapolis, IN., 1990, originally published in 1964) pg. 47

resting with the people is a form of idolatry, for Allah's word, as given through Muhammad, is regarded as the only legitimate source of legislation, and in addition, obedience to Allah's law is the only form of worship Islam allows. These two ideas: that the divine is a law giver, and that obedience to that law is what constitutes worship, are the two most alien concepts confronting the western mind when analyzing Islam, even though the former exists to some degree in Judaism. They combine to create the Islamic requirement for territorial sovereignty, something entirely unique among the world's religions. According to Islamic doctrine, if a Muslim obeys the laws of man, as he must while residing in a modern western state for example, he actually worships man and becomes an idolater guilty of *shirk* – worshipping other than the one god, Allah. This is a grave sin for a Muslim and so to atone he must engage in the struggle against jahiliyya, which is to say, all non-Muslim culture and ideas, as these are thought to arise out of ignorance of the truth of Islam. And since Islam disallows criticism of itself, it forms a completely closed system of thought with all definitions, including the definition of freedom, self-contained. Qutb puts it plainly:

> "Since the objective of Islam is a decisive declaration of man's freedom, not merely on the philosophical plane but also in the actual life, it must employ jihad. It is immaterial whether the homeland of Islam – in the true Islamic sense, *dar al-Islam* – is in a condition of peace or whether it is threatened by its neighbors. When Islam calls for peace, its objective is not a superficial peace requiring only that part of the earth where the followers of Islam are residing remain secure. The peace of Islam means that *din* (i.e., the law of the society) be purified for Allah, that all people should obey Allah alone, and every system that permits some people to rule over others be abolished. [2]
> (...)
> "Thus, this struggle is not a temporary phase, but an eternal state, because truth and falsehood cannot coexist on this earth. Whenever Islam made the universal declaration that Allah's Lordship be established over the entire earth and men be free

---

2 Qutb, Sayyid, *Milestones* (American Trust Publications, Indianapolis, IN., 1990, originally published in 1964) pg. 51

from servitude to other men, the usurpers of Allah's authority on earth have struck out against it fiercely; they never tolerated it. Islam was obligated to strike back and free men throughout the earth from the clutches of these usurpers. The eternal struggle for the freedom of man will continue until all religion is for Allah and man is free to worship and obey his Sustainer."[3]

Consider the phrase, "truth and falsehood cannot coexist." This is a central concept in Islamic thought – that everything "false" must be destroyed. Therefore, all other cultures, when having come under Islamic domination are eventually annihilated by Islam, including their art, music, books, cultural artifacts of any kind, and of course history, all must be obliterated because these things are un-Islamic and are thus deemed worthless. Cultural genocide is what jihad in all its forms (propaganda, demography, bribery, extortion and finally violence) seeks to accomplish because these things are obstacles to the realization of perfect Islam. Again quoting Qutb,

> "The reasons for jihad...are these: to establish Allah's authority on earth; to arrange human affairs according to the true guidance provided by Allah; to abolish all the Satanic forces and Satanic systems of life; to end the lordship of some men over others, since all men are creatures of Allah and no one has the authority to make others his slaves or to make arbitrary laws for them. These reasons are sufficient for proclaiming jihad. One should always keep in mind, however, that there is no compulsion in religion; that is, once the people are free from the lordship of men, the law governing civil affairs will be purely that of Allah, while no one will be forced to change his beliefs and accept Islam." [4]

Central to this argument is the idea that Allah's sovereignty must be realized over actual physical territory, for one of his essential attributes is as legislator for the collective. The idea of God's will reign-

---

3 Qutb, Sayyid, *Milestones* (American Trust Publications, Indianapolis, IN., 1990, originally published in 1964) pg. 53
4 Ibid. pg. 57

ing over the heart of the individual believer, the kingdom of heaven within, is an alien one to Islam and considered by Muslims to be a corruption of the truth.

In this collectivist religion the individual cannot attain happiness and fulfillment apart from the functioning of the collective, because freedom is only found through the complete submergence of the individual in this social, political and religious system.

This is the opposite of our conception of happiness as individual self-realization, or, the actualization of individual potential. In Islam, peace is only found through the total loss of individuality in complete obedience to the system. When, at some future time, when every human being is living exactly the same way, praying at exactly the same times, and repeating exactly the same words while doing so, then and only then, will Allah be satisfied and mankind become justified. Human happiness per se, is never considered and the attainment of perfection is a purely collective act. Allah deals only with the ummah, never the person (since Muhammad) or the personal. Human purpose is found only in conformity.

The concept of the kingdom of heaven being spiritual in nature and individual in manifestation is unrecognized by the material religion of Allah. *"For the light shown in the darkness and the darkness comprehended it not."* The efforts of Muslims to co-opt Christianity (Jesus as a "Palestinian" Muslim and slave of Allah) reveals perhaps a fear of dealing with the words of the Jewish carpenter on their own terms. Ignorance of Christianity among ordinary Muslims is nearly total and of course kept that way by the intimidation and even killing of missionaries and the banning of bibles and other Christian materials in Muslim controlled lands. Muslims often assert that most of the words of Jesus as recorded in the New Testament are corrupt fabrications but that Christ foretold the coming of Muhammad. When Jesus spoke of the "Comforter" or the "Spirit of Truth" also known as the Paraclete, Christians understand this to be a spiritual presence, but Muslims construe this to mean an actual human being, Muhammad.[5] This underscores once again how Islam elevates the material over the spiritual.

In the western mind, in order for freedom to exist, evil or the

5 Ibn Warraq, "Koranic Criticism 700 C.E. to 825 C.E." *New English Review* October 2007

potential for evil must also exist, otherwise freedom, as we conceive it, is impossible. Man must be free to choose between the true and the false, between reality and his own delusions. In point of fact, human delusion, that is, the willful embrace of unreality, is undoubtedly the greatest source of evil in the world. And non-Muslims can easily recognize the unreal nature of the mythical ummah and how it is entirely analogous to the mythical communist collective or the mythical Third Reich, projected both backward and forward in time. Here again is Qutb sounding remarkably like Karl Marx,

> "After annihilating the tyrannical force, whether political or racial tyranny, or domination of one class over the other within the same race, Islam established a new social, economic and political system, in which all men and women enjoy real freedom." [6]

In truth, however, man walks a tightrope between the spiritual prison of conformity to the mores (the doing of only what is accepted and expected) and the prison born of his own personal selfishness and the desire for unreality. The cultivation of self-control then is indispensable to true freedom as recognized by all the major world's religions. With self-control, human actions are forced neither by the sensual appetites nor by fear of social or divine retribution. Self-mastery becomes the key to both peace and freedom because it opens up the possibility of personal choice based on individual self-reflection. Forced conformity as found in Islam can only kill individual faith even as it claims to liberate man through obedience to Allah's system. This is clearly not merely delusional, but dangerously so.

Real faith is in fact the great emancipator, for faith properly defined is the actual living connection between the individual believer and his divine source of love and life. Through faith we feel God's presence and are able discern his will, to know right from wrong, righteousness from sin, and truth from falsehood. Faith is the mechanism that allows man to search for God, which is to say, to search for reality. Islam, on the other hand, is the destroyer of faith and the bestower of

6 Qutb, Sayyid, *Milestones* (American Trust Publications, Indianapolis, IN., 1990, originally published in 1964) pg. 49

48

delusion, creating nothing but the most profound unhappiness, born of absolute self-denial, among its adherents. The idea that God would actually desire human happiness is utterly foreign in Islam, for according to its doctrine, Allah does not value the individual except for his contribution to the collective. The idea that the individual personality has value in and of itself is non-existent. Thus art, as it is born of unique individual thought, cannot be valued, much less treasured or preserved. Islam means everything, the individual Muslim means nothing except as a vehicle for the spread of Islam. His life, his loves, his suffering, his joy, means nothing except as it relates to Islam. Islam uber alles. Islam forever. Islam, Islam, Islam.

So what the Islamic system has done is usurped the place of God in the lives of its believers. It has made a spiritual God unnecessary. The Islamic system is all one needs to know and obey. One must memorize the fixed words of the Qur'an, but knowing God as a living spiritual being is not required. It is not even considered. Muslims may only look forward to lives of bitter self-denial or lives culminating in self-annihilation. The actual faith adventure of finding God, being liberated by his love and growing to know him is denied them. The freedom Muslims are promised is of course entirely delusional because the reality in Islam is a life reduced to utter slavery - physical, psychological and spiritual – without balm, without rest, without peace. We witness its fear-driven fanaticism every day in final proof that religion reduced to politics and faith reduced to conformity, cannot take the place of true religion or supplant true religious faith without dire consequences. Let us compare the following two quotations:

> "When one shakes the hand of a *Kafir*, and smiles in their face, it takes away a part of their [sic] *al-Walaa wal Baraa*; it weakens their [sic] hatred against the *Shirk* of the *Kafir*. Nowadays, for Muslims in the West, they have total love for the *Kafireen* by showing it in their expressions and actions. They are a people who are strangers to the '*Aqeeda of Ahlus Sunnah wal Jama'ah* since we are required to show open hatred for the *Shirk* of the *Kuffar*." [7]

7 Quoted from the Muslim website
http://www.inshallahshaheed.wordpress.com

"But I say unto you, Love your enemies, bless them that curse you, do good to them that hate you, and pray for them which despitefully use you, and persecute you" – Matthew 5:44

The question is: what is the proper response to the institutionalized hatred of non-Muslims promoted by Islam? How do we do as Jesus commanded and love our enemies while at the same time acting to prevent our culture and civilization from being destroyed? How do we return good for evil and repay hatred with love? Can it be done? Or even more urgently, should it be done?

The attempt by Muslims to equate Islam with a perceived inherent "muslimness," that is in turn derived from the idea of superiority/inferiority of men's souls that is central to Islam, has caused a great deal of confusion. In Western culture the equality of souls before God is taken for granted and indeed forms the basis for our concept of equality before the law. Taken to extremes, the ideal of legal equality can be used to attempt to erase all kinds of social differences. But the metaphysical is the only sense in which total human equality exists in Western thought regardless of the attempt by some to substitute social equalitarianism for the ideal of democracy. Nonetheless, equality before the law underlies all our ideas of social fairness.

Islamic law, on the other hand, is built upon the idea of the inequality of men; that there is an inherent difference between the Muslim and the non-Muslim at the deepest level, and these must be treated differently in order for society to be fair and just. This concept forms the basis of Muslim social thought and is also the basis for Muslim supremacism and likewise forms the basis of Muslim social cohesion.

The root of Western social cohesion lies in the idea of the Fatherhood of God and its corollary concept of the Brotherhood of Man. Though not unique to Jesus, this Judaic concept formed the basis of his teaching: all men are sons of God and therefore all men are brothers in the spiritual sense. We owe a duty to our brothers above and beyond that owed to other relationships. And by serving our brethren we thereby serve God.

So the question becomes, how do we best serve our Muslim brethren? Are they served by our failure to acknowledge what are, to us, the obvious errors and shortcomings of Islam? Are they served by allowing the barbarism enshrined in Sharia Law to spread in the world so that more and more human beings are trapped within it? Are they served when we allow Muslim women and girls to be handled as property? Are they served by allowing the essentially materialistic nature of Islam to trump the imperatives of value? Are they served when we dispense with honest judgments under the guise of impartiality?

Compassion demands that we see Muslims as human beings first, and if we acknowledge them as children of God, we must acknowledge that God's love for Muslims is in every way equal to his love for us, for God's love is infinite and indivisible. That love then places certain demands upon us. Should we not then thoroughly examine the fundamental error of Islam, that is, of seeing the world's peoples as divided and fundamentally separate, that Muslims and non-Muslims are not only different, but Muslims are more and non-Muslims less? If God's love is divided, then God who is love must be divided, and though Muslims claim otherwise, that they worship "one God," their theology in this regard is contradictory and insupportable.

Judged in this light, is it not incumbent upon us to seek to free individual Muslims from the totalitarian thought-system of Islam, just as we once sought to free Eastern Europeans from the totalitarian system of communism on the basis that it is fundamentally in error? And are not Muslims triply enslaved, in body, in thought and in spirit by the insurmountable boundaries and incessant demands of Islam? It should be obvious that peace does not come from living in a spiritual prison. Peace in the spirit can only be attained by the active seeking of a new and better way, not by fatalistic submission to the *only* way.

Muslims know, and expressly let us know, that our beliefs and even our very existence form a threat to Islam because we represent freedom of thought and believe ourselves perfectly free to declare Muhammad not to be a prophet nor a figure fit for emulation. This is psychologically intolerable to Muslims who cannot admit such thoughts into their own minds for then they might come to the realization that everything they have known all their lives is in error. Previously solid ground turns to quicksand, and so they attempt to destroy the source or sources of that thought, and see threats to Islam closing in from all directions, so great is their fear. Put simply, any criticism of Islam is a threat to Islam.

On our side, a clear distinction must be made between Muslims as individual human beings and Islam as a belief system. Opposing communism was never equated with hatred of the people living under communist rule and so it must be understood with Islam as well. There is no reason opposition to Islam should be equated with any form of hatred, for we understand Muslims are truly an enslaved people. We seek only to free them from this tyranny and allay the deep spiritual suffering caused by Islam, and we do this from the most altruistic of motives, that of love and concern for Muslims as human beings; human beings who are trapped, through no fault of their own, in a totalitarian system of physical, mental and spiritual repression. We should seek to break the hold Islam has on the Muslim mind.

Leadership in this vein is difficult if not impossible to find, however. "We need to forsake the Christendom model and shed the idea that [Christians] need to promulgate a worldwide Christianity," said Lee Camp, theologian at David Lipscomb University in Nashville, Tennessee on Nov. 28, 2006.

> "The most basic Christian commitment … is that we say we believe in the Lordship of Jesus. But, if we claim that, how can a Muslim or a Jew trust us, if we say Jesus is the Lord of all Lords?" [8]

A firestorm of protest broke out in response to this remark. David Lipscomb is a deeply conservative Church of Christ college and its alumni, parents of students and other concerned citizens rose up in righteous indignation essentially requiring Professor Camp to write "I believe Jesus is Lord" fifty times on the blackboard. He offered his contrition couched in the following defiant terms.

> "The claim of the Lordship of Jesus has often been divorced from Jesus' call to be merciful to those with whom we differ. In fact, the claim has often served as a battle-cry, an imperialistic profession used to destroy Jews and Muslims. In view of this

8 Camp, Lee as quoted by Anita Wadhwani, "Christians must 'let go' some beliefs for sake of peace, theologian says" *The Tennessean* Nov. 29, 2006

history, Jews and Muslims have good reasons for not trusting those who wear the name Christian." [9]

However, it is perfectly clear many people (including this theologian) fear a resurgent Christianity as much or more than they fear a resurgent Islam, but it is dismaying to observe a Christian theologian proposing the preemptive surrender of the right to define God in Christian terms. The definition of God goes to the very core of this struggle, for it in turn defines the nature of civilization. The question is: shall we allow Christ to define himself as the historical record of his life and teachings indicate, or shall we allow Muslims to define him for us as Isa, the "Palestinian Muslim," divorced from Judaism, with no historical foundation for this assertion whatsoever? And furthermore, should we allow Muslims to define themselves as part of the Abrahamic tradition that links Judaism and Christianity when the entire doctrine of Islam repudiates that tradition and fabricates its own history, a replacement history of pure fantasy? I think not. Even Professor Camp in his clarifying essay remarked, "I have long disagreed with those who say that Jews, Muslims and Christians are all 'saying the same thing.' Serious adherents of their respective faiths know this is not the case."

Thus we cannot allow Christ's historical Jewishness to be removed, nor the fact that Christ did not repudiate the Jewish scriptures, but rather spiritualized and expanded them so that Jews and gentiles now share a common heritage, a heritage that forms the basis of Western Civilization, and even that they share hope for the realization of the Brotherhood of Man, the Kingdom of Heaven as realized on earth. The prayer the Master left us includes the words, "thy kingdom come, thy will be done on earth as it is in heaven," and this in turn is based on the understanding that God's will is good, something utterly foreign to Islam, which doctrine would simply proclaim God's will is. The two are entirely different concepts with entirely different consequences for civilizational progress and direction.

Moreover, it seems obvious that the more religious Muslims become, the further they enter a state of being cut off from the God of tender feelings, those feelings of love for life and appreciation of beauty

---

9 Camp, Lee as quoted by Felicia Benamon, "Compromising Our Christian Faith," *Canadian Free Press* Dec. 20, 2006

that make life worth living, that cause us to feel at home in the universe and part of humanity. On the contrary, Muslims seem to withdraw more and more from reality the more religious they become (dressing in 7th century Bedouin garb, observing 7th century Arabian manners etc.), until the most religious of them offer up the ultimate act of worship in their faith and commit murder or murder/suicide in the name of Allah without feeling any compassion for their victims or for themselves - the ultimate divorce from humanity.

Despite the claim of Islam as being Abrahamic, it is not a religion that teaches that the highest commandment is to love God with all one's heart and one's neighbor as oneself, which comprises the essential morality and forms the basis for Western social cohesion. The highest commandment in Islam is to obey Islam. The reason Islam exists is not to enhance morality or to make life better for its adherents. Rather, Islam seemingly exists only to propagate itself.

One might observe that if a belief system does not enhance morality, true morality, not seen mainly as the regulation of sexual relations (controlled as yet another aspect of tyranny), it cannot be a religion in the sense we know religion in the West and we are not obligated therefore to treat it as a true religion. A moral system not based on love is not real morality, but only a list of arbitrary rules.

I believe the proper Christian response toward Muslims is to love them as ourselves, but to act on that love by opposing Islam with all our hearts and minds. Furthermore, we should just as vigorously oppose all Christian leaders who counsel the surrender of Christianity for "peace." If we surrender the historic Jesus, whether we believe him to be divine of not, we surrender truth.

5
Tribalism, Sacrifice and Taboo

Historically, war has been of two kinds. One kind of war has been a simple contest over land and power: who will control what? But the last two great wars of mankind, the Second World War and the Cold War, were something else: a contest between two differing views of reality or possibly two levels of reality comprehension involving two differing levels of morality. War as a contest of military strength was part of, but only part of, what was an existential ideological struggle. And sometimes two parties on the same side, allies, may have fought together, against a common enemy, for different reasons. The Soviet state was totalitarian, and the Russians who fought the Germans did not do so as defenders of liberal democracy, but as defenders of the Russian land, and in so doing, inflicted terrible damage on the Germans. The Americans and British and those in the Resistance movements were fighting the Nazis because the Nazi world view was *wrong* and as such, could not be allowed to prevail. Similarly, we fought the Communists during the Cold War, resisting and attempting to weaken them in every way because the communist worldview, with its simplistic conception of the nature of man, was wrong. And being in error, these worldviews led to injustice. Both ideologies held a view of man and his place in the universe that was narrow, material and ultimately immoral. It was not just the Nazi or the Soviet war machines that had to be defeated; it was the Nazi and the communist ideas and their implication for human existence that threatened Western civilization.

We fought both World War II and the Cold War in large part to *bring the enemy to his senses.* To make him admit the error of his thinking and to stamp out the cruel injustice these worldviews inflicted upon humanity. This was war within the Western tradition, but it was war to answer the vital core questions, what is man and what is his purpose on earth? Man's relation to the state was actually a secondary consideration.

Now we find ourselves fighting a war in order to answer the

question, what is God and what is man's relation to him? We might also state the question this way: what is reality and what is man's relation to it?

Recently, many people in positions of influence have made the decision that the answer to this question is unimportant; that life as such is more valuable than the spiritual, emotional and mental life in which human life is lived. To preserve life is all. And therefore to fight for truth or justice, if it means the destruction of life, is immoral. The credo, "Give me liberty or give me death" must be incomprehensible to such timid souls who would preserve their lives and avoid war as all costs.

Political liberty is one thing, but spiritual liberty, because it is intangible, is difficult to define and even harder to fight for. Many statesmen, clergymen, and academics are advising us to abandon the fight before it is fully joined by purposefully minimizing the stakes involved. There is no question the belief system of Islam creates a very different culture which in turn creates a very different society and in turn creates a very different political system than the Christian belief system creates. This is so because human culture is not a product of the forces of nature, but is a creation of the human mind. Minds believing in differing non-tangible realities will naturally create different cultures, societies and political systems.

The struggle between the two different answers to the questions "what is God (or reality) and what is man's relation to him (or it)?" that Islam and Christianity represent will likely determine the future course of human existence. It certainly is a contest that has not stopped for over 1300 years, and there is no natural end to it, given that the belief-system of Islam is unlikely to change. Muslims come pre-equipped to the battle because they are taught Christianity is wrong, and that Christian doctrine perverts the truth. Christians, on the other hand, are disarmed at the start and are in fact taught not to criticize another's religion. Islam, according to most Christians these days, simply cannot be wrong. Its teachings are often polar opposites from Christian doctrine, even so, modern Christians maintain Islam must somehow be right too and that there must be common ground to be found and compromises to be made that will avert the reality of the war we find ourselves in. "Must be," in this context, is a form of pretence masquerading as belief.

Former British Prime Minister Tony Blair often spoke about a "war of ideas" but allowed on our side only a demonstration of our "faith in tolerance" with the vague idea that Muslims have "faith in tolerance" also and so common ground can be found there. Blair also demonstrated a profound confusion between virtue and value. In an article in *Foreign Affairs*, Blair speaks about his faith that values are something to be demonstrated rather than defined:

"We knew that you cannot defeat a fanatical ideology just by imprisoning or killing its leaders; you have to defeat its ideas.

"We will not win the battle against global extremism unless we win it at the level of values as much as that of force. We can win only by showing that our values are stronger, better, and more just than the alternative.

"This is ultimately a battle about modernity.

"This is a battle of values and for progress, and therefore it is one that must be won. If we want to secure our way of life, there is no alternative but to fight for it. That means standing up for our values, not just in our own countries but the world over. We need to construct a global alliance for these global values and act through it.

"In my nine years as prime minister, I have not become less idealistic or more cynical. I have simply become more persuaded that the distinction between a foreign policy driven by values and one driven by interests is wrong.

"Globalization begets interdependence, and interdependence begets the necessity of a common value system to make it work. Idealism thus becomes realpolitik.

"That is why I say this struggle is one about values. Our values are our guide. They represent humanity's progress throughout the ages. At each point we have had to fight for them and defend them. As a new age beckons, it is time to fight for them again." [1]

By leaving the word "value" vague and undefined an attitude is revealed that could only be described as being based on the fear of discovering anything that might contradict his premise. If Prime Minister Blair allowed that his premise, common ground in common values, could be false, then he would have to admit to himself and before history that he has foolishly based his entire foreign policy on the shallowest form of analysis and one that has been nurtured and sustained by wishful and insipid thinking.

With the breakdown of religion in the modern world, there is consequently great confusion over what faith really is and a consequent retreat into childish reasoning based on what seems to be confusion between believing and pretending.

True faith is demonstrated by those who fight on the side of truth against that which is untrue. Faith is belief in the reality of Truth. Faith is trust in Truth. Faith is betrayed when one pretends something is true when it is not.

In the Western world religious belief is demonstrated by trusting in moral forces that are unseen, but nevertheless conceived of as real. These forces are thought to be outside the self and as such are not subject to individual control. The robust faith of a full grown adult seeks to adjust the self to reality, not reality to the self. God, in other words, is not mocked.

When we pretend, on the other hand, we project imaginary control out onto the world. An adjunct to this is the thought that to ignore the reality of evil is to deny it power. This kind of thinking is prevalent in everything from Christian Science to the New Age movement and all manner of mental therapy books in between. The thinking is that to acknowledging evil somehow causes it to bloom into reality as though human beings have the creative power of little, magical gods and is analogous to the reasoning of children. Children often think if they believe in something hard enough, it will come true.

Unbelievably, this kind of childish reasoning holds sway at the

1 Blair, Tony, "A Battle for Global Values" *Foreign Affairs* Jan./Feb. 2007

highest levels, not only of government, but of academia as well. Diana Eck, professor of comparative religion at Harvard University, should be competent to make comparisons between religions and one would expect her to do so, yet here she is in the Boston Globe advising that comparisons be ignored:

> [On interfaith dialogue] "The point is not to agree, not even to find common ground, but rather to learn to listen through their differences. Most important, they build lasting friendships…
>
> "Interfaith dialogue is not happy hand-holding premised on agreement. It is the kind of encounter we need to understand our deepest differences and build a society that bridges them."[2]

What Professor Eck seems to be saying is that society can be made to cohere on the basis of individual friendships alone and that these friendships needn't be based on any common understanding about the nature of man, or the nature of reality. Even though Muslims believe on the deepest level in a fundamental inequality between Muslims and non-Muslims, Eck maintains this can somehow be bridged if we "listen through the differences" which must mean ignoring those differences.

So here we have a professor of comparative religion, at Harvard University no less, advocating not comparing religion. Would any student graduating from her classes be able to make scholarly comparisons between Christianity, Judaism and Islam? I doubt it. Islam seems to be the subject she is avoiding at all costs.

Eck insists, "the first step in learning about Islam should be meeting our Muslim neighbors." Really? Would it do for a professor teaching a class on Christianity to advocate grabbing a random Christian off the street and asking him about it? What about the historical texts? Islam is an entirely text-based religion. It doesn't matter what Muslims think it is or say it is: it simply is. Islamic doctrine consists of a collection of texts: the Qur'an, the Hadiths and the Sira, and Is-

---

2 Eck, Diane L., "Good neighbors" *Boston Globe*, Dec. 24, 2006

lam is a religious, social and political system based upon those texts. Islam is not the Muslim people. Just as Christianity is not the Christian people.

In the Western tradition going back to ancient Greece we recognize three absolute values, truth, beauty and goodness. In practical life, these absolutes act somewhat like yardsticks by which we may intuitively measure those qualities in objective reality. Other values are derivative or are the product of the association of the basic three. Virtue, on the other hand, may be thought of as the "fruit of the spirit," the natural, personal result that occurs when a man places his faith in the reality of these values. Virtues are personal qualities such as patience, temperance, meekness, humility, forbearance and yes, tolerance. Tolerance may be valued, but it is not a value in itself.

The tolerance spoken of within the context of Islam is, like many things, wholly communal. Muslims as a group tolerate the existence of non-Muslims as a group so long as each of those non-Muslims adheres to certain Islamic laws while living under Islamic domination (which is the God-given, natural order of mankind), such as payment of the poll tax to the Muslim polity, among other economic, social, and legal disabilities endured by those non-Muslims.

The word tolerance, then, has two very different meanings in the context of the two cultures. When former PM Blair speaks of "respect for tolerance" as common ground between the Jewish, Christian and Muslims religions, he knowingly, or perhaps unknowingly, buys into Muslim propaganda; propaganda that pushes forth words and concepts that mean one thing to Western man, but quite another to Muslim man. Some other examples are the words: "justice," "peace," "faith," "prayer," "worship," "prophet" and "Abrahamic." Though the words are the same, they convey entirely different meanings to Jews and Christians on the one hand, and to Muslims on the other. Most Muslims, I believe, are aware of this difference. Most Jews and Christians, however, are not.

Nor are most Christian Churches helping Christians to define these differences so as to defend Christianity and Western civilization. Often the clergy consider the role of "peacemaker" to be that of obscuring those differences in the same manner Diana Eck and Tony Blair do. Karen Armstrong, an ex-nun, has emerged as one of the primary lay apologists for Islam[3] and the Archbishop of Canterbury, Rowan Williams, regularly excoriates the Western world for the self-inflicted misery of the Islamic one and the Archbishop has even described Islamic law to be "unavoidable" in Great Britain.[4] Christ's injunction for the individual to suffer injustice by "turning the other cheek" has been transformed into a model for civilizational non-defense by numerous well-meaning would-be peacemakers who are unwittingly aiding the enemy by counseling surrender. The history of the decline and fall of Eastern Christianity is filled with such well-meaning fools.[5]

Real peacemaking is the result of the stout and unyielding defense of the values our civilization was founded upon. We can start by defending the truth concerning the differences between Islam and Western civilization. We can attempt to bring the enemy to his senses (non-violently) by pointing out the errors in his understanding of reality, because the truth is, Islam is deeply and profoundly *wrong*. Pretending it is right only worsens our situation by delaying actions that must be taken if our own civilization, however imperfect and unseemly it may be, is to be preserved.

True and lasting peace will not come through the betrayal of the truth or through deliberately ignoring reality. Peace in Islam, for Believers, is seen as the Peace that will reign when the last obstacle to the spread of Islam is removed. But obstacles to the spread of Islam to our own peoples is exactly what must be insisted upon. A race is on, between those who insist upon, and preach to others, comforting illusions, and those who stonily insist on seeing things as they are. For the latter, much of what is happening is disquieting but as a famous Englishman once wrote, the mind can only repose on the stability of truth. In all the confusion, those who see things aright remain grimly unconfused.

A few years ago, before the attacks of 9/11, it seemed the world was moving toward increased integration, with our loyalties correspondingly expanding to embrace ever greater swaths of humanity. In

3 See Armstrong, Karen, *Muhammad: A Prophet for our Time* (Eminent Lives imprint of HarperCollins, New York, 2006)

4 BBC News Feb. 7, 2008 http://news.bbc.co.uk/2/hi/uk_news/7232661.stm

5 See Ye'or, Bat, *The Decline of Eastern Christianity Under Islam* (Fairleigh Dickinson University Press, New Jersey, 1996)

the period from the founding of the American Republic up to the Civil War, American loyalties had at first been given to states and regions. Indeed, the Articles of Confederation, which were adopted in 1786, were finally given up because they provided for a central government without the power to tax, without the power, that is, to withstand the long-established power of the states. The Civil War did not do away with the enduring Federal system by which we are both citizens of states and of a nation, but did end forever, or so we thought, the idea that one's loyalty to state or region might rival, or even surpass, loyalty to the nation.

Modern Europe consists of established nation-states, each with its own history, culture, language and literature. After two disastrous world wars, the first disastrous in the loss of life, the second in the loss of both life and morale, Europe needed to find a way, or thought it did, to make sure that such events were never repeated. Nationalism was deemed the culprit and so two supra-national organizations were formed, the UN and the EU, in order to integrate the nations of the world and create the means for peaceful conflict resolution.

It seemed possible at that time to envision world wide integration with an international government to take care of international affairs, a national government to care for national affairs, a state government for state affairs and local government to govern local affairs and so forth – all to be democratically chosen by the people, of course. The elimination of warfare itself seemed to be within reach and a government of mankind, by mankind and for mankind a real possibility in the coming generations. All this seemed to require was the transference of individual loyalty to larger and larger groups. Nationalism seemed to be a dying anachronism: we would be citizens of the world, owing allegiance to all mankind and warfare would be a thing settling into the dustbin of history.

Instead, after a very long lag – just the way at the end of World War I, the "war to end all wars," may have been followed by the Briand-Kellogg Pact "outlawing war," which pact had dozens of signatories by the time Adolf Hitler came to power, and started a systematic program of German rearmament, and by the time the Japanese were making plans to take, and had taken part of, what they then called Manchukuo (Manchuria) – again we see the reemergence of ethnic identity as a force in the world.

Today the rivalry between China and the United States looks more and more like the Great-Power rivalry between England and Germany in 1912. The menace of Islam has already weakened the Atlantic Alliance, and helped to split America from Europe. That menace now has caused the United States to expend large sums, and to focus almost all of its attention, on ways to deal militarily with a threat that, for now, is not primarily a military one, but a matter of ideology and demography.

And there was another force at work during this same post-war period: that of multiculturalism, which was, then as now, actively seeking to weaken the internal cohesion of Western nations, and more importantly, Western culture, by removing what Richard Weaver calls the "tyrannizing image" of Christianity. The problem is that without this strong and polarizing ideal, culture and society is left with nothing to adhere to, no natural morality and nothing which creates order. So much so, that today a new tribalism is emerging in our midst.[6] Barack Obama wrote in his memoir, *Dreams from My Father* published in 1995, this description of black student life at Occidental College in Los Angeles:

> "There were enough of us on campus to constitute a tribe, and when it came to hanging out many of us chose to function like a tribe, staying close together, traveling in packs... It remained necessary to prove which side you were on, to show your loyalty to the black masses, to strike out and name names.

> "To avoid being mistaken for a sellout, I chose my friends carefully. The more politically active black students. The foreign students. The Chicanos. The Marxist professors and structural feminists."[7]

For Obama, embracing American culture would be to "sell

6 See Derbyshire, John "Will The United States Survive Until 2022?" *New English Review* Jan. 2007

7 Obama, Barack as quoted by Bill Sammon "Trapped between two worlds" *The Examiner* Jan. 30, 2007

out," so he embraced the forces seeking to undermine what was to him a "foreign" culture. This is America in the 21st Century.

In the Islamic world, where the ideal loyalty is to the worldwide Islamic community as a whole, the reality is that loyalty to the nation-state is constantly undermined and tribalism continually returns as the ever-present the fall-back position. Sunni and Shia loyalties today are quickly supplanting loyalty to individual Muslim nation-states, beginning with, but not ending with, Iraq, nation-states which are in any case regarded as a western imposition. It goes without saying that no state can remain standing long which cannot command the loyalty of its people.

One is reminded that quite recently in the 19th Century, the failure of the American Indians to form a true nation-state and thus quell their crippling internecine tribal warfare was perhaps the major cause of their disastrous defeat at the hands of the much more highly organized and integrated American state. Islam, having no concept of the nation-state whatsoever, will forever be host to internecine tribal warfare and will not be strong enough to command loyalties of disparate groups in those Muslim countries, such as Iraq or Lebanon or even Pakistan, where Shi'a as well as Sunnis exist in large numbers, or as in Sudan or Algeria or Morocco or Iraq, where non-Arabs live in large numbers together with Arabs. This is not a situation the West should deplore however, as Hugh Fitzgerald has been continually and patiently pointing out over the last several years. [8]

A primary function of the nation-state in the West is to preserve and defend Western culture. And culture is a direct creation of mind, actually an accretion over time of a series of minds, and in the Western world those minds have largely been formed by, until quite recently, religious ideals that come out of a long Judeo-Christian tradition. Western culture, then, is an outgrowth of the religious ideal; that which men hold to be of the highest spiritual value. As discussed earlier, Western Christian culture is based on the conception of God as a benevolent, dependable and loving father and of the universe as containing an inherent moral order. Hinduism, Buddhism and Confucianism also hold to the conception of a morally ordered universe that

---

8 See for example Fitzgerald, Hugh, "What Did The Bush Administration Not Know (About The Sunnis and Shi'a) And When Did It Not Know It" *New English Review* Aug. 2006

is discoverable by the human mind.

Islamic culture is centered around a very different, but equally strong and polarizing idea. Morality in Islam is not found through the individual embrace of progressive value; the discovery of ever greater truth, beauty and goodness. Instead, morality is set down in the unchanging and unchangeable doctrine of Islam, which to the Western mind appears wholly arbitrary with the exception of one overriding principle: that which perpetuates and promotes Islam is moral, while that which weakens Islam is immoral. Islamic doctrine is the ideal around which the Islamic culture is organized. Muslims consider Western concepts of good and evil as simply abstract notions. The only "reliable" way Muslims distinguish the two is by referral to the doctrinal texts. The Qu'ran, Hadiths and Sira are quite literally "all ye know and all ye need to know" on earth for believing Muslims. The concept of religious progression is anathema, and is thought to be the road to corruption. As Richard Weaver writes,

> "A culture then is a complex of values polarized by an image or idea. It cannot be perfectly tolerant or even tolerant to any large extent because it lives by homogeneity. It therefore has to exclude on grounds which are cultural and not "rational" what does not comport with its driving impulse." [9]

This is certainly true of Islamic culture, based as it is on the sacrifice of the individual in favor of the group and mainly concerned with its own perpetuation. The individual does not matter; his proper place is to submit to Allah and not even to question whatever rules have been laid down by Allah – rules as to what is prohibited, and what commanded, for "Allah knows best." The believer must accept even that which might offend his sense of reason or of goodness. His willingness to submit is the sole measure of his righteousness, and he is required to ignore the workings of reason, or of one's sense of right and wrong that might transcend, or even differ from, official Islamic doctrine – say, the rules pertaining to women, or the hostility and even hatred directed at non-Muslims who may here and there be tolerated if they fulfill their

9 Weaver, Richard, *Visions of Order* (Louisiana State University Press, 1964, republished by Intercollegiate Studies Institute, New Jersey 1995) pg. 20

duties as non-Muslims under Muslim rule, but there is no room for individual thought, questioning, or imposing values or hierarchies or judgments on the rules set down by Allah, expressed in the Qur'an, and made further sense of by what Muhammad himself did or said. Whatever helps Islam is moral, whatever allows for the spread of Islam is good, whatever helps the forces of Islam to dominate everywhere, and to ensure rule by Muslims, is similarly good by that very fact. It makes sense. It coheres. It would be strange if the total ideology of Islam, which is far more than a religion prescribing rituals or offering an explanation of creation, but an attempt to organize and regulate every area of life, did not have such a result.

By contrast, the Western religious ideal operates primarily on the individual (who then influences the culture) and is to a great extent dependent on the temperament, cultural background and personal experience of the believer. Western religious sects rest ultimately on the spiritual experience of an individual or individuals. As William James pointed out, religion is so vital to human experience that, as we discovered in the case of communism, it cannot be legislated away or forced out of existence.[10] Religion is an essential part of the human experience. The problem is, religion may be a force for good or a force for evil, depending on what is venerated.

Muhammad is regarded by Muslims as having brought the final revelation, and so all other revelations, including the auto-revelation of the individual, are generally not tolerated. The Islamic religion cannot change; therefore the Islamic culture cannot permanently change, though it may accept the products of non-Muslims, that is, of the modern world, it cannot change in its underlying values. It must either expel or force conformity on all that is not Islamic in order for Muslim society to integrate culturally. And Islam is a master integrator. In *Visions of Order*, Richard Weaver explains:

> "In speaking of culture's power to influence and to bind I have more than once used the word "integrate," since a culture is something unitary gathered about the dominating idea. But "integration" and "segregation" are two sides of the same op-

---

10 See James, William, *The Varieties of Religious Experience* (New American Library, New York, 1958)

eration. A culture integrates by segregating its forms of activity and its members from those not belonging. The right to self-segregate then is an indispensable ground of its being. Enough has been said to show that our culture today is faced with very serious threats in the form of rationalistic drives to prohibit in the name of equality cultural segregation. The effect of this would be to break up the natural cultural cohesion and to try to replace it with artificial politically dictated integration. Such "integration" would of course be a failure because where deep inner impulse is lacking cohesiveness for any length of time is impossible. This crisis has been brought to our attention most spectacularly in the attempt to "integrate" culturally distinct elements by court action. It is, however, only the most publicized of the moves; others are taking place in areas not in the spotlight, but all originate in ignorance, if not in a suicidal determination to write an end to the heritage of Western culture."[11]

Indeed it would seem that in the contest of cultures we find pressed upon us, so surprisingly, and so unexpectedly, Western culture continues to be engaged in the process of active self-dismemberment. We in the West are denying to ourselves the one essential element of self-determination, that of segregating and expelling that which does not conform to Western cultural standards. There are some things the West cannot tolerate and expect to survive. Certainly the inequality of women under the law, including polygamy and enforced dress, is one of those things. But there is so much more in the alien and hostile creed of Islam which cannot be assimilated, nor tolerated, by a Western society that wishes to remain intact.

Of those human impulses lying at the base of religion, and thus at the base of culture, the urge to sacrifice is one of the most primordial. Sacrifice originates in the idea of man being born in forfeit to the gods, born in original sin. He owes the gods something in return for his continued existence, or continued prosperity, or continued happiness and success. The thought that the wrath of God must be assuaged is very ancient. Think of Agamemnon's attempted sacrifice of his daughter Ip-

11 Weaver, Richard, *Visions of Order* (Louisiana State University Press, 1964, republished by Intercollegiate Studies Institute, New Jersey 1995) pg. 21

higenia so to obtain a favorable wind for his fleet. Man is engaged in perpetual bargaining with God.

God was, and indeed still is, thought to demand some kind of payment for his favor. We in the West substitute for direct sacrifice; we tithe to our churches and synagogues, but the concept that God will reward the payee for this payment by directing the contribution back "tenfold," or that the payee will be rewarded by God in some other manner, is born of an ancient and primitive religious bargaining impulse.

Man is constantly seeking to balance the books with God by thanking him through sacrifice in times of plenty, or by sacrificing in order to receive God's favor in times of scarcity or turmoil. This thinking has given rise to other rituals of propitiation, such as Catholic confession, performed in order to appease the wrath of God upon the commission of sin, or ritualized prayer to thank God for his bounty, and so forth. The urge to self-sacrifice may also be prerequisite to all our ideas of saintliness. But added to this and underlying all this, is still the individual relationship with, and communication with, God. Western Religion is, at bottom, a personal experience for which ritual is only an aid, not an end in itself.

In Islam, on the other hand, sacrifice and ritual fill the entire horizon. There is little or no room for personal religious experience and little tolerance for personal bargaining with God. Allah is not courted by the soul, but rather is obeyed through the bodily obedience to Islamic doctrine, which is in itself an all-encompassing sacrifice. There is no allowance for exceptions. The mujahadeen, or warriors for Allah, who sacrifice their all for Islam in order to destroy the enemies of Islam, are the closest thing Muslims have to saints; saints all cut from the same cloth, the form of Islamic martyrdom.

As civilization progressed, the primitive urge to sacrifice either to please or appease the gods eventually grew into group renunciation which developed into societal taboos, (thou shalt not...). Taboos, in their turn, made laws, built social institutions and remain important elements in cultural cohesion. The religious taboos in Islam are part of a highly developed system, so much so, that permitted vs. not-permitted (halal vs. haram), are carried close to absolute levels through the imposition of draconian punishments, such as stoning for adultery. As a cultural segregator, Islam has no equal. It is ruthless in excising that which is not-Islam, and this, of course, is a key to its success.

In order for the Western world to effectively deal with Islam, it must also be a ruthless segregator and expel that which is not-West, in this case, the cultural practices of Muslims. For practical purposes this may mean putting policies in place that reverse the current demographic trends of Muslim immigration into Western lands.

At this point, it is useful to remember that all war results in the movement of peoples. The mass movements following WWII were perhaps the largest in human experience, when ethnic Germans were expelled from all over Eastern Europe. Sometimes these expulsions were a matter of government decree, as in Czechoslovakia through the Benes Decree, while others moved in response to the social pressure exerted by their neighbors. But the fact remains, millions were uprooted from the territories of Poland, Russia and Czechoslovakia to be resettled into the then shrunken German homeland. They endured hardship, starvation, disease and death. The transfer could have been handled more humanely, but it was necessary they be moved. Indeed, had they been moved before the advent of the war, it is doubtful Hitler could have launched his invasions as quickly and effectively as he did, and thus the actual shooting war may well have been less devastating in the end.

It seems we have come to a crossroads. We have the choice either to minimize the current threat and the numbers of people bearing it in the West, and then to contain that threat within certain boundaries outside our nations, or we can continue with business as before, as the states and elites of Europe continued to do all through the 1930s, through the re-militarization by Hitler of the Rhineland, and the enormous German rearmament, and the Munich capitulation, and the Anschluss hysteria, until the invasion of Poland, which finally created a situation impossible to ignore, and both Britain and France went to war. And by that time, the Germans were too strong, had been allowed to become too strong with no counter-measures, just as the Japanese had been ignored in East Asia, and all that was left was the outcome we all know: total, devastating war.

If total war is to be avoided this time, populations of those who cannot conceivably assimilate, whose motivating beliefs makes them permanently hostile to Western political and legal and social institutions, and who, in ways we cannot always fathom or predict, may now be, or if not now may later become, or their children may become if they remain devout Muslims, threats to our physical security and our national security and will require constant, very expensive monitoring. Our sentimental belief that everyone wants the same thing, and that all creeds are essentially the same, will no longer do, and the kind of preemptive population transfers undertaken by Czechoslovakia (and many other European states), after World War II, when the Volksdeutsche were sent to Germany, will have to be considered, discussed, and ultimately, have to take place in a perfectly rational, no-nonsense, unhysterical and humane way. Recent decades have seen all kinds of population transfers (Hindus and Muslims, Greeks and Turks, Jews and Arabs), and also simple expulsions, especially by Muslim countries: Libya with Egyptians and "Palestinians," Saudi Arabia with Yemenis, Kuwait with "Palestinians," Iraq with Egyptians and so on. It can be done.

Total war is not inevitable. A few wise, though politically difficult, steps taken now will do much to avoid a much greater catastrophe, likely to be visited on our children, if we do nothing.

6
The Myth of Equality

One of the most striking results of modern democracy has been the gradual but steady erosion of all classes of distinction and the subsequent leveling of society to the point where everyone is expected to treat everyone else in exactly the same way. We must make no distinction between young and old, male or female, distinguished or dissolute. As a result, common courtesy is at an all time low and an unhealthy reservoir of resentment at an all time high. Every person suspects he is not receiving his due and is suspicious that deference in the form of courtesy on his part will be mistaken as submission. Authority is suspected to be nothing but the unfair abuse of power and yet people seem to be seeking true sources of authority amid the ruling relativism by following fads and the ever-changing gurus of the self-help industry. The pressure to conform to pop-culture standards is also immense, so much so, that individuality itself is threatened.

The entire eighteenth century revolt of the rationalists against hereditary privilege and ecclesiastical power is crystallized in the founding document of the United States, specifically the Declaration of Independence, in which human equality was first described by Thomas Jefferson as "sacred and undeniable" and subsequently changed by Benjamin Franklin to "self-evident," substituting reason alone for Jefferson's religious sentiment of sacredness. The result was our founding myth: human equality. And yet, true equality is discovered only on the highest level of transcendence in the sense that our souls, quivering and naked, will someday stand equal before God. On the material level, obviously, and at the risk of sounding trite, no two human beings are alike and are therefore unequal. Furthermore, the ideal of liberty dictates that a certain kind of inequality, social and economic, shall increase, rather than decrease, over time. The ideal of equality militates against liberty and exerts pressure toward conformity in the direction of mediocrity.

While it is true that justice requires equality before the law (in this sense, just as in Islam, the law is a stand-in for God), if the state should attempt to treat every person completely equally, the result is injustice for all, coupled with the gradual lowering of standards for all. When the ladder of cultural distinction (once constructed of virtue and wisdom) is removed, mankind is thrown back into an animal level of materialism where force and money are power and power alone rules. Hierarchy will still exist, but it will be based on the crudest of criteria, appetites and passions. And as the common man is increasingly celebrated, the trend in all aspects of public life, the arts, literature and music, will tend inexorably toward mediocrity.

The modern dismissal of honorifics, even disposing of Mr. and Mrs., on down to the shortening of names is indicative of the modern attitude toward the individual "Dick and Jane." Human beings are now routinely discussed in terms of units of consumption and production. As consumers we are analyzed and dissected as to preference and taste as no other people in history. Our politicians prostrate themselves before the idol of The Economy and continually churn out programs designed to cushion the already complacent middle class, a class whose purpose in life seems to be that of busy consumption.

Rather than engendering happiness, this loss of place in society for the individual has led to resentment, envy, suspicion and bitterness. It seems there was actually less resentment in an ordered hierarchical society than one in which distinction is removed. The peasant and artisan, soldier and tradesman, priest and aristocrat, all knew their places and could easily interact with courtesy and without shame. To work with ones hands at a satisfying craft is an enobling experience which has been largely erased from modern life along with agrarian pursuits. Inflated titles have increased as has the drudgery of work life. And the strong sense of belonging that used to come from fulfilling a vital role in society is missing: the butcher, the baker, the candlestick maker are gone now, replaced by giant concerns employing the cheapest and most expendable labor possible. As a result, the bonds of trust and loyalty between men have been loosed.

We live with a dichotomy where class mobility in term of economics is fluid, but the ladder to other kinds of distinction has been removed and replaced with the emptiest of measures: one's bank balance. Virtue is suspected of being a conspiracy to cheat people of their rightful share of pleasure and wisdom has been pushed aside by overgrown children in their University playpens, the academics who push knowledge toward ever greater specialization and dissociation.

Underneath it all is a simmering cauldron of potentially explosive resentment. As Richard Weaver put it, "If we attach more significance to feeling than to thinking, we shall soon, by simple extension, attach more to wanting than to deserving."[1] Stanley Kurtz explored one outlet for this resentment, Black Liberation Theology, in National Review:

"James H. Cone, founder and leading light of black-liberation theology, is the Charles A. Briggs Distinguished Professor of Systematic Theology at Union Theological Seminary, New York. [Barack Obama's pastor, the Rev. Jeremiah] Wright acknowledges Cone's work as the basis of Trinity's perspective, and Cone points to Trinity as the church that best exemplifies his message. Cone's 1969 book *Black Theology and Black Power* is the founding text of black-liberation theology, predating even much of the influential, Marxist-inspired liberation theology that swept Latin America in the 1970s. Cone's work is repeatedly echoed in Wright's sermons and statements. While Wright and Cone differ on some minor issues, Cone's theology is the first and best place to look for the intellectual context within which Wright's views took shape.

"Cone credits Malcolm X — particularly his famous dismissal of Christianity as the white man's religion — with shaking him out of his theological complacency. In Malcolm's words:

The white man has brainwashed us black people to fasten our gaze upon a blond-haired, blue-eyed Jesus! We're worshiping a Jesus that doesn't even *look* like us! Oh, yes! . . . The blond-haired, blue-eyed white man has taught you and me to worship a *white* Jesus, and to shout and sing and pray to this God that's *his* God,

---

1 Weaver, Richard, *Ideas Have Consequences* (University of Chicago Press, 1948) pg. 37

the white man's God. The white man has taught us to shout and sing and pray until we *die*, to wait until *death*, for some dreamy heaven-in-the-hereafter ... while this white man has his milk and honey in the streets paved with golden dollars here on *this* earth!??

"In the late 1960s, Malcolm X's criticisms (Wright calls them "devastating") were adopted by the founders of the black-power movement, such as Stokely Carmichael, the Black Panthers, and Ron Karenga. Shaken by Malcolm's rejection of Christianity and taken with the movement for black power, Cone, a young theologian and initially a devout follower of Martin Luther King Jr., set out to reconcile black power with Christianity. He did not reject Malcolm's disdain for a "blond-haired, blue-eyed Jesus" — rather, he came to believe that Jesus was black, and that an authentic Christianity, grounded in Jesus's blackness, would focus with full force on black liberation. Authentic Christianity would bring radical social and political transformation and, if necessary, violent revolution in the here and now." [2]

In an obvious parallel to Islam, Black Liberation Theology divides the world between black and white, in the same way Islam divides the world into believer versus non-believer. Black Liberation Theology can even be said to subvert Christianity by erasing the basic Christian concept of the Fatherhood of God and the subsequent concept of the brotherhood of man and replacing this obligation for brotherly love with an obligation to hatred. This is Christianity turned upside down and a real question exists as to whether this kind of belief system should be considered Christian at all.

There is also a question as to whether if, in the mainstream Christian churches, the zeal for equality has not replaced the much more fundamental concept of brotherhood. Brotherhood carries responsibilities simple equality does not. With brotherhood the focus is on others, with equality the focus is on oneself. The resulting egotism that pervades modern society is well laid out in Theodore Dalrymple's

2 Kurtz, Stanley "The God of Black Power" *National Review* May 19, 2008

book, *In Praise of Prejudice,* and need not be gone into here, but it may be commonly observed that when equality is raised to such heights as to destroy all sources of authority, mankind quickly reverts to the animal level of might makes right.

Whereas equality militates against distinction and authority, fraternity does not do this. Brotherly affection is unaffected by varying levels of capacity and ability and this is as it should be. Fraternity is a much superior concept upon which to base society than a mythical and unattainable equality. Society may treat different men fairly, but it cannot treat all men equally without destroying the very structure of society. Society must have structure, or it does not exist. Mankind becomes simply a mass of individual economic units and the only thing separating them is economic success, the natural result of the Darwinian state.

Culture, on the other hand, is a uniquely human product. It is not the simple result of economic causes and effects. It is the creation of human imagination, the result of a shared metaphysical dream. That dream has been maintained by belief in a loving Creator who desires all his children to love one another as brethren. We are losing that dream and the culture that has been its creation, largely as a result of the contending myth of equality.

Furthermore, observing contemporary philosophical trends, one may discern two opposite and contending views of reality which chiefly concern the location and genesis of evil. One the one hand, is the traditional Judeo-Christian view, but which may also encompass, broadly speaking, Oriental traditions such as Confucianism, Taoism and to some extent, Buddhism, which locate the origin of evil internally, that is, within the selfish human heart. In this view, man is born with the potential both for good and for evil within himself. It is the task of the mind to distinguish and then choose between these contending tendencies or principles through contact with the outer world, and by making decisions within that reality, to move toward the good and eliminate the evil internally. In this way character is developed and the soul made more solid and real. On the other hand, is the viewpoint that man is born in innocence and essential goodness and that it is outside forces which primarily engender evil and cause internal discord. In this view, the human decision-making process mainly concerns distinguishing good from evil in exterior reality, and thus the intention and effort to do good in the world is the primary factor determining righteousness and well-being. On this side, Islam rests squarely along with material secularism but, there is a marked tendency in many Christian churches and Jewish synagogues toward this viewpoint as well. A good summary of the first viewpoint is found in John Milton's *Areopagitica*:

> "Assuredly we bring not innocence into the world, we bring impurity much rather: that which purifies us is trial, and trial is by what is contrary. That virtue therefore which is but a youngling in the contemplation of evil and knows not the utmost that vice promises her followers, and rejects it, is but a blank virtue, not pure; her whiteness but an excremental [superficial] whiteness ... Since therefore the knowledge and survey of vice is in this world so necessary to the constituting of human virtue, and the scanning of error to the confirmation of truth, how can we more safely and with less danger scout into the regions of sin and falsity than by reading all manner of tractates and hearing all manner of reason? And this is the benefit which may be had of books promiscuously read." [3]

The concept of "purity" in Islam is almost entirely material. It concerns strict material conformity to Islamic ritual and strictures (thought to be the embodiment of God's will), but largely leaves the interior world, which is such a focus of Eastern and Judeo-Christian thought, alone. Morality and conformity are one and the same in Islam. And the source of impurity is thought not to lie in the human heart, especially not the Muslim heart (only Muslims are thought to be born in innocence while non-Muslims are born in guilt), but in forces outside; thus the focus on female virginity and the fear touching "unclean things" (pork, dogs, urine, feces, dead bodies, non-Muslims, etc.). The thinking is these material contacts affect the soul and its destiny.

By contrast, in the Western tradition of opposing superstition, "There is nothing from without a man, that entering into him can defile

3 Milton, John, "Areopagitica" in *The Complete Poetry and Essential Prose of John Milton* (Edited by William Kerrigan, John Rumrich and Stephen M. Fallon, Modern Library, New York, 2007) page 939

him: but the things which come out of him, those are they that defile the man."[4] In other words, according to Jesus, it isn't what goes into a man's mouth, but rather what comes out, that makes him unclean. He was ever concerned with the inner man, not with ritual (this remark came in response to criticism of his failure to observe ritual washing) or outward displays of piety and it is this emphasis on personal inner purity and morality, or rather on the effort made toward inner purity, that has characterized the Western moral tradition ever since.

For those who drift along with the prevailing modern tendency to locate the source of evil in the outer world, many feel a strong social responsibility to stamp out corruption wherever it may be found so that it may not spread iniquity among the populace. (This concept is especially strong in Islam.) Those people, like the bureaucrats making up the various Human Rights Commissions, now sprouting all over the Western world, think of themselves as fighting evil and protecting society, even if by doing so they reduce grown men to the status of children. Who can forget the interrogation of Ezra Levant before the Alberta Human Rights Commission and how he refused to assume the position of a child, instead insisting on his freedom as a publisher and as a man to examine the news of the Muslim riots over the Muhammad cartoons (and to publish the source of that controversy – those very cartoons) as he, a newspaperman, saw fit? [5]

The Alberta Human Rights Commission (and several others, notably the British Columbia Human Rights Commission which heard the case against Mclean's magazine and Mark Steyn) seeks to impose a middle ground between two diametrically opposed systems of thought in the interest of social harmony. They do so using the excuse that the act of publishing these mild cartoons, which were the cause of worldwide violence and threats of further violence by Muslims, or that of pointing out, with alarm, the current demographic trends in Europe, would directly cause prejudice against Muslims in Canada. In short, they seek the suppression of speech and the press in order to promote social harmony and create in society the virtue of temperance. As Milton writes,

---

4 The Bible, Mark 7:15 King James version
5 See http://ezralevant.com/

"How great a virtue is temperance, how much of moment through the whole life of man! Yet God commits the managing so great a trust, without particular law or prescription, wholly to the demeanor of every grown man…God uses not to captivate under a perpetual childhood of prescription but trusts him with the gift of reason to be his own chooser." [6]

Islam is emphatically opposite: God does give law to man to make him temperate and to create a perfect utopian society; and the fact is, material secularism provides no basis with which to argue that virtue should not be encouraged or even prescribed by law. At the same time, "human rights" are imagined to be some kind of absolute and yet an absolute without any logical grounding in transcendent absolutes. They just "are" in the way that the catagories of haram and halal just "are" in Islam - a basis of morality, and yet, when two "human rights" contend, as in this case, where the right to freedom of the press and freedom of speech come up against the right not to be offended which is almost, at least according to the HRCs concerned, indistinguishable from the right not to be discriminated against on the basis of religion, then, if the goal is to make both rights compatible, one or the other must bend. Thus, human rights are not absolute at all and can easily be erased "at the drop of a law." [7]

Another problem with the effort to modify a fundamental human right like freedom of the press and freedom of speech is there is no practical stopping place of restraint between complete freedom and total suppression, as explained by Alexis de Tocqueville:

"If anyone could point out an intermediate and yet a tenable position between the complete independence and the entire servitude of opinion, I should perhaps be inclined to adopt it, but the difficulty is to discover this intermediate position. Intending to correct the licentiousness of the press and to restore the use of orderly language, you first try the offender by a jury;

---

6 Milton, John "Areopagitica" in *The Complete Poetry and Essential Prose of John Milton* (Edited by William Kerrigan, John Rumrich and Stephen M. Fallon, Modern Library, New York, 2007) pg. 938

7 See Dalrymple, Theodore, "Who Cares?" *New English Review* (August 2006)

but if the jury acquits him, the opinion which was that of a single individual becomes the opinion of the whole country. Too much and too little has therefore been done; go farther, then. You bring the delinquent before permanent magistrates; but even here the cause must be heard before it can be decided; and the very principles which no book would have ventured to avow are blazoned forth in the pleadings, and what was obscurely hinted at in a single composition is thus repeated in a multitude of other publications. The language is only the expression, and if I may so speak, the body of the thought, but it is not the thought itself. Tribunals may condemn the body, but the sense, the spirit of the work is too subtle for their authority. Too much has still been done to recede, too little to attain your end; you must go still farther. Establish a censorship of the press. But the tongue of the public speaker will still make itself heard, and your purpose is not yet accomplished; you have only increased the mischief. Thought is not, like physical strength, dependant on the number of its agents; nor can authors be counted like the troops that compose an army. On the contrary, the authority of a principle is often increased by the small number of men by whom it is expressed. The words of one strong-minded man addressed to the passions of a listening assembly have more power than the vociferations of a thousand orators; and if it be allowed is the same as if free speaking was allowed in every village. The liberty of speech must therefore be destroyed as well as the liberty of the press. And now you have succeeded, everybody is reduced to silence. But your object was to repress the abuses of liberty, and you are brought to the feet of a despot. You have been led from the extreme of independence to the extreme of servitude without finding a single tenable position on the way at which you could stop.

(...)

"In this question, therefore, there is no medium between servitude and license; in order to enjoy the inestimable benefits that the liberty of the press ensures, it is necessary to submit to the inevitable evils it creates. To expect to acquire the former and escape the latter is to cherish one of those illusions which commonly mislead nations in their times of sickness when, tired with faction and exhausted by effort, they attempt to make hostile opinions and contrary principles coexist upon the same soil." [8]

Certainly, when we Americans gaze across the Atlantic, we see many nations "in their times of sickness" which seem to have lost their way, are confused, and forgetful of their own origins and identities. They have been uprooted from their Christian past and material secularism provides no defense against parasitic Islam. Secularists claim to be able to find the answer in human rights, but as we have seen, if these rights are not grounded in transcendent value, they are meaningless. Milton argues that freedom of expression is given by God and can therefore not be removed without transgressing the divine mandate. Freedom of expression is freedom of thought and thought and imagination are the only means mortal man has to escape crushing material reality. Freedom of thought is where real freedom lies. But, even if the authority of Christ is removed, there are still more arguments to make in favor of freedom of speech and the press that can be derived from common sense knowledge of human beings. Milton put it best:

"[I]f it be true that a wise man like a good refiner can gather gold out of the drossiest volume, and that a fool will be a fool with the best book, yea without a book, there is no reason that we should deprive the wise man of any advantage to his wisdom, while we seek to restrain from a fool that which being restrained will be no hindrance to his folly" [9]

(...)

---

8 de Tocqueville, Alexis, *Democracy In America* Vol. 1 (Henry Reeve text as revised by Francis Bowen, Phillips Bradley editor; Vintage Books, New York, 1945) pgs. 188-9 and 192

9 Milton, John, "Areopagitica" in *The Complete Poetry and Essential Prose of John Milton* (Edited by William Kerrigan, John Rumrich and Stephen M. Fallon, Modern Library, New York, 2007) pg. 943

"If therefore ye be loath to dishearten and utterly discontent, not the mercenary crew of false pretenders to learning, but the free and ingenious sort of such as evidently were born to study and love learning for itself, not for lucre or any other end but the service of God and of truth, and perhaps that lasting fame and perpetuity of praise which God and good men have consented shall be the reward of those whose published labors advance the good of mankind, then know, that so far to distrust the judgment and honesty of one who hath but a common repute in learning, and never yet offended, as not to count him fit to print his mind without a tutor and examiner, lest he should drop a schism or something of corruption, is the greatest displeasure and indignity to a free and knowing spirit that can be put upon him." [10]

There will be those who argue that to regulate speech for the common good is but an inconvenience for the few who would bring disharmony and agitation to the masses and that the majority of people will be blissfully unaffected. However, such turns out not to be the case. Freedom of expression, which is simply the "clothing" of freedom of thought, is the cornerstone and basis of all real freedom and it is exactly that freedom which is targeted by Islam, which, as is widely known, prohibits any criticism of itself by prescribing death for blasphemy (criticism of Islam or Muhammad) and for apostasy (leaving Islam). Thus, if Muslims can succeed in disallowing criticism of Islam in the West through the use of hate speech legislation, they will have effectively bound the Western world philosophically and imprisoned the Western genius, so Islam's ultimate ascendancy will simply be a matter of time. Thus, the line must be drawn at freedom of speech and the press or it cannot be drawn anywhere.

A key strategy for Muslims and their sympathizers is to seek to elevate "freedom of religion" to a level of transcendence over the more fundamental freedom of thought and speech. Of course, the full and free exercise of the Islamic religion, would carry with it the supremacy

---

10 Milton, John, "Areopagitica" in *The Complete Poetry and Essential Prose of John Milton* (Edited by William Kerrigan, John Rumrich and Stephen M. Fallon, Modern Library, New York, 2007) pg. 946-7

of Islamic law over Infidel law and over Infidel territory, a situation the American Founders could not possibly have contemplated. Freedom of thought, and thus freedom itself, would be rendered null and void. When contemplating freedom of religion it is relevant to remember we do not allow many abhorrent practices that have been committed at one time or another during the course of human history in the name of religion. If we go so far as to proscribe certain sacraments, which we do, such as the use of peyote in American Indian rituals, we can certainly proscribe certain doctrines especially one that divides the world and all its souls into mutually hostile camps and advocates hatred and violence on the part of one side against the other. Furthermore, it is important to remember we do not allow the full and free practice of Islam now. To do so would require the exchange of our civilization for theirs.

Nevertheless, the overwhelming tendency in the Western world today is toward the restriction of speech (see Ezra Levant, Mark Steyn, Oriana Fallaci, Geert Wilders, Elisabeth Sabaditsch-Wolff and all those in the future who will undoubtedly come under official censure for speaking their minds about Islam) and just as the ultimate symbol of the previous Dark Age was the Inquisition (even though those Inquisitions actually occurred later), we may fully expect a new Dark Age to be ushered in by a new Inquisition which, just like the previous one, will be conducted in the name of equality and for our own good.

7

The Decline of Christianity & Idealism

Despite what seems to be incessant criticism of Christianity today, the reality is there is really very little real criticism of specific Christian doctrine, criticism that would help to correct the course of modern Christianity. Growing ranks of militant atheists rail against religion as a whole and call for its complete abandonment. Religionists in turn find themselves forced to defend religion in its entirety and are distracted from what might be profitable religious self-criticism. In addition, many Christian congregations have taken up social causes as they have gradually abandoned the cause of religion as such. Furthermore, the general decline of religion has led to an increase in superstition even among the highly educated and more than a few congregations are directly involved in fostering superstitious thought.

Instead of feeding the Lord's sheep in the spiritual sense, many churches justify their existence by pointing instead to their "good works." Generally, these works involve "helping the less fortunate," not spiritually, but materially. Spiritual ministry is either a secondary consideration or is being abandoned altogether and so many churches are becoming simply agencies of social reconstruction. Both the manner of this reconstruction and its goals go unexamined because the sanctity of the churches is involved. Most people assume their church wouldn't be sponsoring this or that social program if it wasn't "for the best," and because these programs make so many people feel good about doing good, it is almost impossible to change the course of these programs or to question their goals.

In many cases, an extension of the church will transform itself into a "volag" or volunteer agency which can then receive remuneration from the government for its good works. In the case of refugee resettlement, these churches receive a cash payment on a per capita basis which creates a financial incentive for the church to sponsor as many refugees as possible. And though many churchgoers feel good about helping "the less fortunate" in this way, the overall effect of bringing

83

large numbers of people, often completely alien to our way of life, and the effect that has on our cultural continuity and our own well being is ignored. The church is seen to be "ministering to the poor" and that's what brings in donations.

Then there is the question of political affiliations. Churches are becoming more and more enmeshed in politics on both sides of the political spectrum. Many church leaders seem more comfortable speaking of politics than discussing religion. They often justify these entanglements with bits of self-serving scripture. As the Archbishop of Canterbury, Rowan Williams, said the "Church has the responsibility and the capacity to ask some fundamental questions about political society and community," and that is true, but speaking as Archbishop, Williams himself pontificates incessantly on political issues. He preaches a political morality with absolute assurance when, for example, he presumes to lecture Israel on the limits of its rights to self-preservation, but when he actually encounters the realities of an Islamic society, he is often surprised at how that society doesn't conform to his expectation; thus, like President Bush, he reveals the full extent of his naiveté. In Pakistan, for example, he was "surprised by how the extremely small Christian minority there is perceived as so deeply threatening by an overwhelming Muslim majority which ought to be more confident and generous about its identity."

On the other side of the political spectrum, as is well known, American evangelical congregations frequently align themselves with the Republican Party. Indeed, Republican candidates must actively court the support of evangelical ministers like James Dobson, Pat Robertson and Franklin Graham. These churches are generally anti-abortion, anti-same sex marriage, for the reintroduction of school prayer, and for the teaching of divine creation in addition to natural selection in public schools. All of these stands concern social reconstruction, though they may be based on what is viewed, or interpreted, as spiritual renewal. Obviously, these churches are just as enmeshed in politics as those on the left-wing. Both sides, to a greater or lesser extent, have abandoned the primary mission of religion, the care and fostering of individual spiritual growth. Individual church members may take part in social and political life, but when churches themselves become involved as institutions, they are often reduced to being simply an arm of this or that political movement and are no longer really churches at all though they retain their tax-exempt status.

Many of these churches, because they are no longer actively involved in the refinement of religious doctrine, abandon their role as arbiters of religious truth and even become parties to the advancement of popular superstitions. This is especially evident in groups that promote the idea that if congregants will only give "seed money" to their organization, the sum given will be multiplied tenfold and returned to the giver by miraculous agency. Donations are solicited through "testimony" as to the effectiveness of this disguised voodoo and there is no doubt such a profitable charlatanry shamelessly preys on the most vulnerable.

Another popular superstition which has roots in the works of Mary Baker Eddy (*Science And Health*) right through the works of Norman Vincent Peale (*The Power of Positive Thinking*) and is now popularized by modern pop-religion writers such as Rhonda Byrne (*The Secret*), is the idea that because thought can change reality, simply by thinking the correct thoughts, health and prosperity will be drawn to the thinker like magic. Often this is kind of superstition is wrapped in scientific jargon and referred to as a "universal law," like gravity. One would imagine that in such a scientifically based age, this kind of thinking would be discouraged, but such appears not to be the case. Surprisingly, it is not the scientifically-minded atheists, but conservative Christians who evince the most resistance to magical thinking. As Molly Ziegler Hemingway informs us:

> "'What Americans Really Believe,' a comprehensive new study released by Baylor University yesterday, shows that traditional Christian religion greatly decreases belief in everything from the efficacy of palm readers to the usefulness of astrology. It also shows that the irreligious and the members of more liberal Protestant denominations, far from being resistant to superstition, tend to be much more likely to believe in the paranormal and in pseudoscience than evangelical Christians.
>
> "The Gallup Organization, under contract to Baylor's Institute for Studies of Religion, asked American adults a series of ques-

tions to gauge credulity. Do dreams foretell the future? Did ancient advanced civilizations such as Atlantis exist? Can places be haunted? Is it possible to communicate with the dead? Will creatures like Bigfoot and the Loch Ness Monster someday be discovered by science?

"The answers were added up to create an index of belief in occult and the paranormal. While 31% of people who never worship expressed strong belief in these things, only 8% of people who attend a house of worship more than once a week did.

"Even among Christians, there were disparities. While 36% of those belonging to the United Church of Christ, Sen. Barack Obama's former denomination, expressed strong beliefs in the paranormal, only 14% of those belonging to the Assemblies of God, Sarah Palin's former denomination, did. In fact, the more traditional and evangelical the respondent, the less likely he was to believe in, for instance, the possibility of communicating with people who are dead.

"This is not a new finding. In his 1983 book "The Whys of a Philosophical Scrivener," skeptic and science writer Martin Gardner cited the decline of traditional religious belief among the better educated as one of the causes for an increase in pseudoscience, cults and superstition. He referenced a 1980 study published in the magazine Skeptical Inquirer that showed irreligious college students to be by far the most likely to embrace paranormal beliefs, while born-again Christian college students were the least likely.

"Surprisingly, while increased church attendance and membership in a conservative denomination has a powerful negative effect on paranormal beliefs, higher education doesn't. Two years ago two professors published another study in Skeptical Inquirer showing that, while less than one-quarter of college freshmen surveyed expressed a general belief in such superstitions as ghosts, psychic healing, haunted houses, demonic possession, clairvoyance and witches, the figure jumped to 31% of college seniors and 34% of graduate students.

"We can't even count on self-described atheists to be strict rationalists. According to the Pew Forum on Religion & Public Life's monumental "U.S. Religious Landscape Survey" that was issued in June, 21% of self-proclaimed atheists believe in either a personal God or an impersonal force. Ten percent of atheists pray at least weekly and 12% believe in heaven."[1]

It could be that much of what we think of as religion occurs on an unconscious level. There are many people currently dedicated to the eradication of poverty, disease, or illiteracy who evince a truly religious zeal for their projects, even though their motives may be unrecognized as such. This unconscious manifestation of a religious drive is difficult to locate, let alone criticize. So rather than benefitting from honest criticism, religion is manifesting itself as an unexamined force which is changing our world in ways we do not always fathom.

The liberal arm of religion is unmistakably becoming increasingly focused on works rather than faith. Doctrine is murky and ill-defined. Never is this attitude made more plain than in Barack Obama's speeches. It is clear he views Christianity primarily as a vehicle for social reform and not much else, as in this speech delivered in 2006 on religion:

"After all, the problems of poverty and racism, the uninsured and the unemployed, are not simply technical problems in search of the perfect ten point plan. They are rooted in both societal indifference and individual callousness - in the imperfections of man.

"Solving these problems will require changes in government policy, but it will also require changes in hearts and a change in minds. I believe in keeping guns out of our inner cities, and that our leaders must say so in the face of the gun manufactur-

1 Hemingway, Molly Zeigler "Look Who's Irrational Now" *Wall Street Journal* September 19, 2008

ers' lobby - but I also believe that when a gang-banger shoots indiscriminately into a crowd because he feels somebody disrespected him, we've got a moral problem. There's a hole in that young man's heart - a hole that the government alone cannot fix.

(...)

"But what I am suggesting is this - secularists are wrong when they ask believers to leave their religion at the door before entering into the public square. Frederick Douglas, Abraham Lincoln, Williams Jennings Bryant, Dorothy Day, Martin Luther King - indeed, the majority of great reformers in American history - were not only motivated by faith, but repeatedly used religious language to argue for their cause. So to say that men and women should not inject their "personal morality" into public policy debates is a practical absurdity. Our law is by definition a codification of morality, much of it grounded in the Judeo-Christian tradition.

"Moreover, if we progressives shed some of these biases, we might recognize some overlapping values that both religious and secular people share when it comes to the moral and material direction of our country. We might recognize that the call to sacrifice on behalf of the next generation, the need to think in terms of "thou" and not just "I," resonates in religious congregations all across the country. And we might realize that we have the ability to reach out to the evangelical community and engage millions of religious Americans in the larger project of American renewal.

"Some of this is already beginning to happen. Pastors, friends of mine like Rick Warren and T.D. Jakes are wielding their enormous influences to confront AIDS, Third World debt relief, and the genocide in Darfur. Religious thinkers and activists like our good friend Jim Wallis and Tony Campolo are lifting up the Biblical injunction to help the poor as a means of mobilizing Christians against budget cuts to social programs and growing inequality.

"And by the way, we need Christians on Capitol Hill, Jews on Capitol Hill and Muslims on Capitol Hill talking about the estate tax. When you've got an estate tax debate that proposes a trillion dollars being taken out of social programs to go to a handful of folks who don't need and weren't even asking for it, you know that we need an injection of morality in our political debate.

"Across the country, individual churches like my own and your own are sponsoring day care programs, building senior centers, helping ex-offenders reclaim their lives, and rebuilding our gulf coast in the aftermath of Hurricane Katrina."[2]

It was in this speech that Obama accused his listeners: "Folks haven't been reading their Bibles," implying that if we had, we would know what terrible things are contained in them and stop pointing fingers at the terrible things in the Qur'an. He also proclaimed America "no longer just a Christian nation; we are also a Jewish nation, a Muslim nation, a Buddhist nation, a Hindu nation, and a nation of nonbelievers." In response, Hugh Fitzgerald wrote:

"As a nonbeliever, I am happy to withdraw any formal claim to the United States being a "nation of nonbelievers" if I must do so in order to prevent, in the slightest way, recognition being given to this nation being "also...a Muslim nation." And I suspect that many Jews, many Buddhists, many Hindus, would be happy to do the same.

"In any case, as a matter of history -- and what is a nation if not that nation's history? -- the United States was founded by, settled by, developed by, Christians or those who thought of themselves, in some cases, as embodiments of the Hebrews, building Zion on a Hill in, of all places, the Massachusetts Bay

2 Obama, Barack "Call to Renewal Keynote Address" Washington D.C. June 28, 2006

Colony (for more on this, read Oscar Handlin). It is truthful to call this nation "Judeo-Christian" in its origins and its mental makeup; it is untruthful to claim otherwise." [3]

Like Rowan Williams, the Archbishop of Canterbury, Obama views Jesus as a social revolutionary, an earlier and more effective William Ayres or Saul Alinsky, and calls the Sermon on the Mount "a passage that is so radical that it's doubtful that our own Defense Department would survive its application." The Sermon on the Mount clearly discusses attitudes and reactions of the spirit and has nothing whatsoever to do with national defense. It seems Obama cannot comprehend what purely religious leadership entails; politics has to be involved, as witness his former pastor for twenty years, the Reverend Jeremiah Wright.

Jesus consistently focused on religion alone, not social, political or economic reform. But it seems those most committed to social reform are eager to use the Master's words to bolster their claims. In fact, Jesus seldom spoke in lecturing tones. His sermons were illustrative rather than informative: "The kingdom of heaven is like..." Often, he taught by asking questions. The Master's final instructions to Peter (who along with Paul is credited with forming the early Christian Church) are illuminating:

"This was now the third time Jesus appeared to his disciples after he was raised from the dead."

Jesus Reinstates Peter (Peter had thrice denied Jesus during his trials.)

15 When they had finished eating, Jesus said to Simon Peter, "Simon son of John, do you truly love me more than these?"
   "Yes, Lord," he said, "you know that I love you."
   Jesus said, "Feed my lambs."
16 Again Jesus said, "Simon son of John, do you truly love me?"

---

3 Fitzgerald, Hugh "America Is Not 'Also A Muslim Nation'" The Iconoclast, *New English Review*, June 24, 2008

He answered, "Yes, Lord, you know that I love you."

Jesus said, "Take care of my sheep."

17 The third time he said to him, "Simon son of John, do you love me?"

Peter was hurt because Jesus asked him the third time, "Do you love me?" He said, "Lord, you know all things; you know that I love you."

Jesus said, "Feed my sheep."[4]

Neither politics, economics nor social reform were part of the Master's explicit mandate for his followers. One can only hope that the churches which proudly bear his name, might humbly begin to comprehend his words and pay heed to his advice, leaving politics at the church door.

Today's accepted wisdom dictates that it really doesn't matter what a man believes in so long as he doesn't take those beliefs too seriously or pursue them too far. In modern usage the words "ideal, idealist and idealism" are all tinged with a hue of unreality. When we describe someone as an "idealist" we do so with that slightly bemused condescension reserved for the overgrown child. We think of idealists as having their heads in the clouds and as being insufficiently grounded in the facts of reality. A pervasive attitude of cynical relativism effectively stifles the striving after any ideal. Yet, it is certainly not what facts a man *knows* that determine his conduct and character, but rather what he *believes*, and the ideals he holds. The decline of idealism, therefore, has not ushered in an era of realism, but one in which guiding principles have gradually been reduced to increasingly superficial standards until there is nothing left but the crudest Darwinian materialism, behaviorism, and genetic determinism as an explanation for the sheer childish selfishness that cloaks itself in the guise of rational self-interest.

This coupling of the ideal with the concept of unreality gained force in philosophical circles seven long centuries ago, but is only now coming into full fruition in society at large. Platonic philosophy had predominated in the Western world for many centuries, advancing the idea that material reality was an imperfect manifestation of spiritual

---

4 The Bible, John 21, 14-18 New International Version

form or the perfect ideal. In this view, the values of truth, beauty and goodness are the comprehensible aspects of transcendent reality – a reality which lies behind or above the material surface we perceive with our senses. William of Occam, however, argued in the fourteenth century that no transcendent reality exists and it is logically unnecessary to propose that it does. Rather these "universals" are simply the product of mental reflection, a necessary result of thought, and are not transcendent over mind or material reality. In the intervening centuries, the world of the senses emerged as the only verifiable reality possible, and anything outside that narrow sphere was banished to the realm of unreality.

In this view, man could be liberated from having to endure the effort to attain ideals, because ideals were thought to be of his own making and could be made and unmade at will. Man could then realize a higher freedom and find ever greater self-realization because he was no longer confined to certain social forms which were all ideals seemed to have become.

The promise of freedom is a mighty lure, almost as strong as the promise of power. Pure logic, liberated from value, seems to provide both. Nature, far from concealing transcendent reality, now seems to contain the mystery of its own genesis as well as its own evolution. Man can break down natural processes through the practice of science, understand how nature works and thus become dominant over the natural world. The thinking is that this will give him power, even over life itself. The great mystery which lies at the heart of existence may be bypassed, or even regarded as superfluous: for it is simply non-utilitarian. In the words of William of Occam, "entities must not be multiplied beyond necessity."

Unfortunately, man underestimated his need for values, because without values, he has no way by which to measure and therefore to judge reality. Logic operates just as well on untrue premises as on true ones and man found that logic alone is not as reliable a path to truth as it first promised to be. The cold logic of Nazism, communism and Islam all operate perfectly well in the absence of truth, beauty and goodness. Values and ideals are the first casualties of a purely logical ideology. In fact, the loss of these ideals may very well prepare the ground for fascism, as men search desperately for something to believe in, some vessel into which to pour their loyalty.

Yet, if the material word holds the secret of life, then by simple extension, wealth and the sensual comfort it provides must hold the key to happiness. American currency, passed down to us from an earlier and sturdier time, is still engraved with the words "In God We Trust," a welcome reminder that trust in money is a foolish act, certain to end in frustration and tears. Warnings ring down through the ages:

> "Will you set your eyes on that which is not? For riches certainly make themselves wings; They fly away like an eagle toward heaven."[5]

> "Do not lay up for yourselves treasures on earth, where moth and rust destroy and where thieves break in and steal;
> but lay up for yourselves treasures in heaven, where neither moth nor rust destroys and where thieves do not break in and steal."[6]

> "So He humbled you, allowed you to hunger, and fed you with manna which you did not know nor did your fathers know, that He might make you know that man shall not live by bread alone; but man lives by every word that proceeds from the mouth of the LORD."[7]

And yet the rot is so deep in American society today that we seem to think we live in a world apart from the natural human condition, a world where property values will rise effortlessly and predictably, where our investments will steadily swell, and where our jobs will remain ever secure as our economy expands forever like the universe itself. This world owes us a living and it is expected of our demagogic politicians to ease our anxiety and boost our confidence in the clocklike regularity and certainty of our mechanistic world. If the machine doesn't run, it is their job to fix it.

Modern man is fond of blaming some person or persons for

5 The Bible, Proverbs 23:5 New King James version
6 The Bible, Matthew 6:19-20 New King James version
7 The Bible, Deuteronomy 8:3 New King James version

everything that goes wrong and will no longer tolerate those who claim there are forces outside his control. Witness the Senate hearings on the economic crisis and their frantic search to find someone to blame, some particular someone who was asleep at the wheel of the great economic machine at the crucial time; someone who should have foreseen that unforeseeable something that, if it had been altered in time, could have prevented the current catastrophe. Witness the effort to assign blame for not preventing the 9/11 attacks or even to blame those attacks on people other than the Muslim terrorists themselves, people more under our control, such as those in the U.S. government. This reflects a primal need to reclaim the certainty that there is nothing outside human direction in the great machine known as the material world. Babies, of course, see themselves as the center of the universe and imagine they are in control of everything. They cry and their needs are met. Have we so elevated wanting over deserving that we have forgotten what maturity means?

Maturity must entail a sense of gratitude for the very hardships so deplored by the young, because it is mainly through adversity that meaningful growth is achieved. Maturity also comes with the growing conviction that it is wrong to live only for oneself and that for life to have value, it must be lived for something greater – for others. Maturity also comes with increasing personal identification with values.

When seasoned by experience, the idealist is an extremely potent force in the world. He is loyal to his ideals to the point of self-effacement. He is not moderate when it comes to virtue or belief. He is an extremist, but not a fanatic. He repudiates the anti-hero and shames the cynic. Consider the following scene, one which can only be described as heroic.

> "Then Pilate entered the Praetorium again, called Jesus, and said to Him, "Are you the King of the Jews?"

> Jesus answered him, "Are you speaking for yourself about this, or did others tell you this concerning Me?"

> Pilate answered, "Am I a Jew? Your own nation and the chief priests have delivered you to me. What have you done?"

Jesus answered, "My kingdom is not of this world. If My kingdom were of this world, My servants would fight, so that I should not be delivered to the Jews; but now My kingdom is not from here."

Pilate therefore said to Him, "Are you a king then?"

Jesus answered, "You say *rightly* that I am a king. For this cause I was born, and for this cause I have come into the world, that I should bear witness to the truth. Everyone who is of the truth hears My voice."

Pilate said to Him, "What is truth?" And when he had said this, he went out again"...[8]

Jesus was obviously not engaging in the "spirit of dialogue." He did not care if Pilate understood him or not, he would not compromise the truth as he saw it; whereas Pilate, in the modern spirit of the true cynic, expressed doubt in the very existence of truth. He asked his question and did not wait for the answer because, like the modern man he represents, truth to him was a relative, fungible commodity. But for Jesus, truth was absolute and his loyalty to truth was likewise absolute.

The man of moderate virtue would be appalled, for it must seem to him that in his refusal to defend or explain himself, Jesus was throwing his life away. Indeed, he handed Pilate ample cause to put him to death. He admitted to being a king: a king in the world of the transcendent surely, but a king nonetheless. Pilate clearly thought Jesus was delusional, but probably harmless. But who in the end should be judged delusional: Pilate, who washed his hands of the affair and went on with his life as though nothing had happened, or Jesus, who went to his death refusing to compromise with evil, loyal to his ideals to the end?

Today, however, we are steadily counseled that solutions to

8 John 18: 33-38 Bible, New King James version

our problems mostly lie in compromise and that there is really nothing worth dying for, actually nothing worth risking much for. "Moderation in all things" is really advice to seek grounds for complacency, to elevate comfort over virtue and to bury our ideals in the graveyard of materialism.

8
The God of History

One of the most confusing aspects of modern Judeo-Christian thought lies in the attempt to reconcile two opposing concepts of God. One is of God as the loving and merciful Father of the individual, who is concerned primarily with individual salvation and survival after death. The other is of God as an actor in history, who controls and shapes the historic drama for his purpose, disregarding the individual, as is often depicted in the Bible. In his book, *After Auschwitz*, distinguished theologian, rabbi and professor of religion, Richard L. Rubenstein proposes that theology itself is essentially an attempt to diminish the cognitive dissonance that belief in both these aspects of God causes in the believer. There is a gulf between the Biblical God of history and the God of human individual experience which theologians attempt to bridge. That gulf has grown wider and those theological bridges less tenable in the face of the unprecedented scale of death and destruction wrought by man in the twentieth century.

In examining this problem it is evident that though God himself must be conceived of as eternal and unchanging, human awareness and understanding of God has been an evolving quest through the generations. The Bible contains a record of the concept of God as it has evolved over the centuries, but is also an historical record of the Jewish people and descriptions of their national drama in which God is thought to take a special interest. This record is traditionally interpreted as that of a God who is involved in reward and punishment of the Jewish people as a whole, chastising them when they stray and rewarding them when they are faithful to his word. The Jews are thought to be held to a higher standard of obedience due to the idea that God has chosen them to be bearers of the divine light.

We are then confronted with the theological problem, not only of flawed divine justice (as all collective punishments and rewards would necessarily be flawed, if not entirely unjust), but also the idea that God must then be involved with evil, even to partake of evil, in order to dispense these collective punishments. So, either God is omnipotent and unjust or he is just but not omnipotent. A third option, that God is self-limited for the purpose of allowing mankind freedom of will, is rarely taken up, for the idea of a punishing God is deeply embedded in both Jewish and Christian thought.

Many Jewish and Christian theologians are of the opinion that God exists in a realm beyond good and evil and that he works his will by using evil as a necessary means to teach and perfect imperfect man, who is ever tending toward selfishness, egotism and greed, and is forever forgetting his obligation to God. In fact, some Jews and Christians even describe the Holocaust as part of the divine plan, that God actually used Hitler in order to punish the Jews. They differ only on the reason for this punishment. Some Jewish theologians have proposed that the Holocaust occurred because the Jews were not faithful enough to the Torah and too assimilated into gentile society (even though the conservative orthodox Polish population bore the full brunt of the atrocities while the more assimilated population in America escaped). Some Christian theologians have surmised that the Jews as a people were still being punished for having rejected Christ (even though the actual rejection of Jesus occurred only on the part of Annas, Caiaphas and a handful of leaders of the Sanhedrin – not the common people, whose very embrace of Jesus had aroused the fear and ire of those same men). Neither of these theological explanations evokes a loving, trustworthy, fatherly God, but rather an anthropomorphic despot, unworthy of enlightened worship. A world in which the creature is on a higher moral plane than the creator poses a theological dilemma of the most profound sort.

The depiction of deity as a vengeful and jealous despot is entirely in keeping, however, with the earliest records of human theological thought as contained in the Old Testament, where man's conception of God began as a tribal deity, chiefly concerned with the welfare of the tribe and one who therefore backed that tribe against enemy tribes which had their own gods. Later, as the concept of deity enlarged, God was envisioned as being the God of all the peoples of the earth and finally of the universe as well.

When Isaiah proclaimed, "Thus saith the Lord, 'Heaven is my

throne, and the earth is my footstool,'"[1] the older Bedouin tribal god of vengeance and jealousy was transformed into a God of transcendent majesty, a universal God ruling heaven and earth. One can easily imagine the emotional need of the people to uphold the idea that even though God has grown larger and is now Lord of all the earth, they who first understood this desired to think of themselves as the nearest to him. "I will take you as my people, and I will be your God. Then you shall know that I am the LORD your God who brings you out from under the burdens of the Egyptians."[2]

Much theological confusion might be avoided if the older conception of God rooted in an ancient tribal deity, a bloodthirsty God who demands sacrifice and appeasement, could be seen as just that, an early human conception of God that can no longer be justified in the modern era.

It makes more sense to understand God as so respecting human free will, that he allows the full consequences of that freedom to reign, if only during man's short time on earth, a time when God's will bows to human will, so that man will be free to choose goodness over evil, truth over error, and the beauty of selflessness over the ugliness of the selfish act. The fact that God allows the tares to grow with the wheat until the harvest, does not necessarily mean that God actively participates in evil or that he is punishing man, only that he is giving mankind a choice.

If it is God's desire to foster courage, faith, loyalty, altruism and devotion within the individual, then the environment man finds himself in must contain danger, uncertainty, betrayal, cruelty and loneliness. He must have an environment in which there is a difference between that which is and that which should be, otherwise there would be no necessity for faith, the reaching for that which is higher and better, for values which lie beyond the material world. There would be no need to reach for God.

We have inherited a tradition in which the higher concepts of God are shackled to those which are lower. In the Christian tradition, we have the idea that God is so bloodthirsty that he was not satisfied with human suffering until he saw his own innocent son dying upon

1 The Bible, Isaiah 66:1 King James version
2 The Bible, Exodus 6:7 New King James version

the cross. And even then he was not satisfied with the suffering of the Jews who, after three millennia of persecution at the hands of the Babylonians, the Egyptians and the Christians, must be further punished for the supreme crime of deicide, even though it was God who required this sacrifice in the first place. The idea that the humanly conceived and executed cold-blooded murder of six million Jews, for the crime of being Jews, could seriously be considered as part of "God's plan" by some Jewish and Christian theologians is appalling. A more stomach-turning conclusion can hardly be imagined. Is there any wonder millions of Jews and Christians are turning away from the old faiths? Cognitive dissonance has reached the breaking point.

Richard L. Rubenstein concludes that we are living through an age of the "death of God." By this, I believe he means the death of the idea, or hope, that God will deal with his chosen people by means of miraculous intervention, that the Jews will have divine protection. This conception was dealt its death blow at Auschwitz. However, there is doubt that without the religious concept of "covenant and election" the Jewish people can survive as a distinct people. It is likewise doubtful whether Christianity can continue in its present form without the idea that Jesus was sacrificed for our sins, but it is equally impossible to believe that Jesus took away the sins of the world with his death. The Holocaust stands as a stunning rebuke to both religious conceptions, making both seem feeble and child-like in the face of such horror.

Furthermore, we are facing theological assault by a religion that claims to restore the original monotheistic concept of God. One which declares that man's conception of God cannot, must not, and shall not evolve. Indeed it would be difficult to imagine a more primitive God. The bloodthirsty Allah delights in the tortures of his hell and rewards those who by slaying his "enemies" by bestowing upon them the sensual delights of a heavenly brothel.

An effective response lies not in clinging to our own more primitive God concepts, but rather in declaring the God concept itself to be one which has evolved and must evolve in order for civilization to be strengthened and renewed.

Perhaps the old God concepts must die before the new may spring forth to take their place. As spoke Jesus, "Most assuredly, I say to you, unless a grain of wheat falls into the ground and dies, it remains alone; but if it dies, it produces much grain."[3]

Dr. Richard L. Rubenstein was recently asked if he thought the Jewish people would ever accept Jesus as a prophet. His answer was an emphatic, "No," explaining that because Jesus, during his Sermon on the Mount, is recorded as teaching by his own authority not always according to the scripture, he cannot be considered a prophet.

> "Ye have heard that it was said of them of old time, Thou shalt not kill; and whosoever shall kill shall be in danger of the judgment:

> "But I say unto you, That whosoever is angry with his brother without a cause shall be in danger of the judgment."
> [4]

> "Ye have heard that it was said by them of old time, Thou shalt not commit adultery:

> "But I say unto you, That whosoever looketh on a woman to lust after her hath committed adultery with her already in his heart." [5]

> "Ye have heard that it hath been said, An eye for an eye, and a tooth for a tooth:

> "But I say unto you, That ye resist not evil: but whosoever shall smite thee on thy right cheek, turn to him the other also."[6]

And he continued,

> "Ye have heard that it hath been said, Thou shalt love thy neighbour, and hate thine enemy.

> "But I say unto you, Love your enemies, bless them that curse

---

3 The Bible, John 12:24 New King James version
4 The Bible, Matthew 5: 21-22 King James version
5 The Bible, Matthew 5: 27-28 King James version
6 The Bible, Matthew 5: 38-39 King James version

you, do good to them that hate you, and pray for them which despitefully use you, and persecute you." [7]

Since none of the other Hebrew prophets did this, according to Dr. Rubenstein's understanding of Jewish theology, Jesus cannot be given prophet status in line with the older Hebrew prophets.

In *After Auschwitz*, Rubenstein also contends that the religious leaders of Jesus' day examined the evidence concerning his work dispassionately and "sadly concluded" that Jesus was not a prophet and his words should not, therefore, be added to the Jewish scripture.

> "At the time of the birth of Christianity, Christians asserted that something decisively new had occurred which had the power to transform the human condition. The Pharisees, my spiritual predecessors, hoped for such a transformation as earnestly as did the Christians. They looked both within and around themselves. They sadly concluded that no such transformation had occurred and there was no alternative but to remain faithful to the Law." [8]

I think the evidence put forward in the New Testament account is different. It shows that Jesus threatened the religious structure which was the source of power and wealth for a few men and it was these men, led by the high priests Annas and Caiaphas, who, in removing Jesus' challenge to their authority, also managed to put an end to serious Jewish consideration of his work. I believe the split between Judaism and Christianity is more accurately described as having been caused by the reaction to Jesus' teaching, rather than having been caused by Jesus himself. And though to many early Christians, Jesus' teaching was radically new especially in comparison with the state religion of Rome, the mystery cults and the cult of Mithras, if we compare his work to that of the earlier prophets, what he brought was not so very different and may be viewed as part of a continuous process in which the concept of God was gradually expanded and enlarged. Jesus built solely upon the

---

7 The Bible, Matthew 5: 43-44 King James version
8 Rubenstein, Richard L. *After Auschwitz, History, Theology and Contemporary Judaism*, second edition, The Johns Hopkins University Press 1966, 1992

existing Hebrew scripture. In the same sermon quoted above, he said:

> "Think not that I am come to destroy the law, or the prophets: I am not come to destroy, but to fulfill."[9]

Let us examine the older prophets and consider whether they too expanded the concept of God and morality in the same way that Jesus demonstrates in the passage above. For it seems to me that Jesus' teaching "by his own authority" is a very tenuous excuse for ruling out the possibility Jesus was a Hebrew prophet and to dismiss the need to consider his teachings in light of that possibility. The older prophets also gave voice to God. Jesus consistently referred to the scripture and constantly referred his authority back to the "Father in Heaven." In the example cited above, he clearly sought to place the older teachings on a higher moral plane, not to overturn them.

There is no better record of the development of religious thought than that contained in the Bible. Like gazing at archeological strata of religious and social development, Biblical stories provide descriptions of life as human beings lived in ancient Israel where they created first a tribe and then a nation; a nation that was destroyed, rebuilt, and then destroyed again. Throughout what is thought to be some twenty centuries of recorded time, from the time of Abraham to the destruction of the Second Temple, one may clearly discern the interplay and interdependence between religion and culture.

It is also important to remember there are vast distances of time between Bible stories. Between the stories of Abraham and those of Moses lie 500 to 600 years and between Moses and the splitting of the Kingdom (not long after Solomon) lie about 300 years and yet another 300 years passed before the Babylonian captivity, for which we have precise dates (between 587 and 539 B.C.).

These holy books were likely put into their present form around the time of the Babylonian captivity after Ezekiel had his visions and the initial shock of defeat wore off. We know they have remained in their present form at least since their translation into Greek in the third century B.C. We also know that after Babylon was conquered by Persia and Cyrus the Great allowed the Jews to return to Jerusalem, the

---

9 The Bible, Matthew 5:17 King James version

temple was rebuilt in 516 B.C. and the Torah was canonized during the 5th century B.C. The scriptures were translated into Greek in the 3rd century B.C. So we know that sometime between the 6th and 3rd centuries B.C. the Hebrew Scriptures came into their present form and have remained so until the present day.

The history of the Jews begins with the story of Abraham, who, once he left the city state of Ur, sometime between the 20th and the 18th centuries B.C., entered a world much like that which still persisted in Arabia in the time of Muhammad. No government functioned outside the cities. Tribal warfare was the rule of the day and each tribe (like each city state) had its own god. There were also household "gods" which must have taken the form of figurines (Rachel stole the household gods from her father Laban's house). These numerous gods were anthropomorphic, angry, vengeful and required constant appeasement in the form of blood sacrifice and burnt offerings. Abraham's is the story of the founding of a tribe and the importance of fidelity to God as demonstrated through faith in him and belief in his word.

> Then the Angel of the LORD called to Abraham a second time out of heaven, and said: "By Myself I have sworn, says the LORD, because you have done this thing, and have not withheld your son, your only *son*— blessing I will bless you, and multiplying I will multiply your descendants as the stars of the heaven and as the sand which is on the seashore; and your descendants shall possess the gate of their enemies. In your seed all the nations of the earth shall be blessed, because you have obeyed My voice."[10]

The tribe was greatly weakened during the Egyptian captivity (which lasted from roughly the 16th Century to the 13th century B.C.) and had to be revived or re-created by Moses after his daring flight. There is evidence not only that the descendants of Abraham, but also many others fled with Moses and so the imperative of that time was the re-establishment of the tribe and the exaltation of the original tribal God, Yahweh. To this end, Moses seems to have utilized the superstitious

10 The Bible, Genesis 22:15-18 New King James version

awe of the people for what must have been an active or semi-active volcano, Mt. Sinai, to emphasize the punishing power of God.

> "Then it came to pass on the third day, in the morning, that there were thunderings and lightnings, and a thick cloud on the mountain; and the sound of the trumpet was very loud, so that all the people who were in the camp trembled. And Moses brought the people out of the camp to meet with God, and they stood at the foot of the mountain. Now Mount Sinai was completely in smoke, because the LORD descended upon it in fire. Its smoke ascended like the smoke of a furnace, and the whole mountain quaked greatly. And when the blast of the trumpet sounded long and became louder and louder, Moses spoke, and God answered him by voice. Then the LORD came down upon Mount Sinai, on the top of the mountain. And the LORD called Moses to the top of the mountain, and Moses went up." [11]

> "Now all the people witnessed the thunderings, the lightning flashes, the sound of the trumpet, and the mountain smoking; and when the people saw *it*, they trembled and stood afar off. Then they said to Moses, 'You speak with us, and we will hear; but let not God speak with us, lest we die.'

> "And Moses said to the people, 'Do not fear; for God has come to test you, and that His fear may be before you, so that you may not sin.' So the people stood afar off, but Moses drew near the thick darkness where God *was*."[12]

There is still an emphasis on sacrifice to appease God's anger and the Ten Commandments were all negative injunctions. Don't do this, or God will punish you. Blood sacrifice and burnt offerings were still required and Moses seems to have ruled with an iron hand to enforce tribal solidarity.

After the reestablishment of the tribe in Canaan, came the

11 The Bible, Exodus 19:16-20 New King James version
12 The Bible, Exodus 20-18-21 New King James version

birth of a real nation. The first of the Hebrew prophets, Samuel, emphasized the power and justice of God. The effect of his teaching was to legitimize the king.

> "There is none holy as the LORD: for there is none beside thee: neither is there any rock like our God.

> "Talk no more so exceeding proudly; let not arrogancy come out of your mouth: for the LORD is a God of knowledge, and by him actions are weighed." [13]

> "The LORD killeth, and maketh alive: he bringeth down to the grave, and bringeth up.

> "The LORD maketh poor, and maketh rich: he bringeth low, and lifteth up.

> "He raiseth up the poor out of the dust, and lifteth up the beggar from the dunghill, to set them among princes, and to make them inherit the throne of glory: for the pillars of the earth are the LORD's, and he hath set the world upon them.

> "He will keep the feet of his saints, and the wicked shall be silent in darkness; for by strength shall no man prevail.

> "The adversaries of the LORD shall be broken to pieces; out of heaven shall he thunder upon them: the LORD shall judge the ends of the earth; and he shall give strength unto his king, and exalt the horn of his anointed." [14]

Amos lived during the time when the kingdom was split into two, the northern (Israel) and the southern (Judah), which occurred in the tenth century B.C. He proclaimed that the Lord would not only punish the enemies of the Hebrew kingdoms, but would punish the children of Israel for their transgressions as well. He proclaimed God

13 The Bible, 1 Samuel 2: 2-3 King James version
14 The Bible, 1 Samuel 2: 6-10 King James version

as Lord of all the nations and declared his justice would come to all, nations and individuals alike.

"Thus saith the LORD; For three transgressions of Judah, and for four, I will not turn away the punishment thereof; because they have despised the law of the LORD, and have not kept his commandments, and their lies caused them to err, after the which their fathers have walked:

"But I will send a fire upon Judah, and it shall devour the palaces of Jerusalem.

"Thus saith the LORD; For three transgressions of Israel, and for four, I will not turn away the punishment thereof; because they sold the righteous for silver, and the poor for a pair of shoes;

"That pant after the dust of the earth on the head of the poor, and turn aside the way of the meek: and a man and his father will go in unto the same maid, to profane my holy name."[15]

"Says the LORD.
   "For surely I will command,
   And will sift the house of Israel among all nations,
   As grain is sifted in a sieve;
   Yet not the smallest grain shall fall to the ground.
   All the sinners of My people shall die by the sword,
    Who say, 'The calamity shall not overtake nor confront us.'"[16]

This assault on the chosen people doctrine was continued by Hosea. While emphasizing the mercy of God, he also stressed the international nature of God.

"And I will betroth thee unto me for ever; yea, I will betroth

---

15 The Bible, Amos 2: 4-7 King James version
16 The Bible, Amos 9: 9-10 King James version

thee unto me in righteousness, and in judgment, and in loving-kindness, and in mercies.

"I will even betroth thee unto me in faithfulness: and thou shalt know the LORD.

"And it shall come to pass in that day, I will hear, saith the LORD, I will hear the heavens, and they shall hear the earth;

"And the earth shall hear the corn, and the wine, and the oil; and they shall hear Jezreel.

"And I will sow her unto me in the earth; and I will have mercy upon her that had not obtained mercy; and I will say to them which were not my people, Thou art my people; and they shall say, Thou art my God." [17]

It was Isaiah, however, who made the transition from a punishing, angry God to a loving, fatherly God. Isaiah seems to have lived after the destruction of the northern kingdom of Israel, which fell to the Assyrians in 751 B.C. and before the Babylonian captivity in 578 B.C. The chronological setting in the first paragraph of his book refers only to the kings of Judah.

"Come now, and let us reason together, saith the LORD: though your sins be as scarlet, they shall be as white as snow; though they be red like crimson, they shall be as wool." [18]

"The Spirit of the Lord GOD is upon me; because the LORD hath anointed me to preach good tidings unto the meek; he hath sent me to bind up the brokenhearted, to proclaim liberty to the captives, and the opening of the prison to them that are bound." [19]

---

17 The Bible, Hosea 2: 19-23 King James version

18 The Bible, Isaiah 1:18 King James version

19 The Bible, Isaiah 61:1 King James version

"I will greatly rejoice in the LORD, my soul shall be joyful in my God; for he hath clothed me with the garments of salvation, he hath covered me with the robe of righteousness, as a bridegroom decketh himself with ornaments, and as a bride adorneth herself with her jewels." [20]

The prophet Micah seems to have lived in approximately the same time. The same kings of Judah, Jotham, Ahaz, and Hezekiah, are listed in his chronological placement paragraph as are listed in the analogous paragraph of Isaiah. Micah prophesied not the victory of the Hebrews over their enemies, but the end of war altogether.

"And he shall judge among many people, and rebuke strong nations afar off; and they shall beat their swords into plowshares, and their spears into pruninghooks: nation shall not lift up a sword against nation, neither shall they learn war any more.

"But they shall sit every man under his vine and under his fig tree; and none shall make them afraid: for the mouth of the LORD of hosts hath spoken it."[21]

Furthermore, he attacked the sacrificial system which was the source of priestly power and wealth, not only for the ancient Hebrews, but for the ancient Egyptians, and ancient Mesoamericans as well. The Christian church also controlled the method of appeasement through the sacrament, confession, penance, intercession of saints and the sale of indulgences during the Middle Ages. Yet, this early prophet of Israel in approximately the seventh century before Christ declared,

"Wherewith shall I come before the LORD, and bow myself before the high God? shall I come before him with burnt offerings, with calves of a year old?

"Will the LORD be pleased with thousands of rams, or with

---

20 The Bible, Isaiah 61:10 King James version

21 The Bible, Micah 4: 3-4 King James version

ten thousands of rivers of oil? Shall I give my firstborn for my transgression, the fruit of my body for the sin of my soul?

"He hath shewed thee, O man, what is good; and what doth the LORD require of thee, but to do justly, and to love mercy, and to walk humbly with thy God?"[22]

Jeremiah lived through the defeat of the kingdom of Judah, the destruction of the first Temple and the taking of the people into captivity at the hands of Nebuchadnezzar, king of the Babylonians in the year 578 B.C. He restored the god of punishment, but for Jeremiah, God is not a national deity. God reigns over all the nations and uses one to punish another. In the passage below, God calls Nebuchadnezzar "my servant."

"And the LORD hath sent unto you all his servants the prophets, rising early and sending them; but ye have not hearkened, nor inclined your ear to hear.

"They said, Turn ye again now every one from his evil way, and from the evil of your doings, and dwell in the land that the LORD hath given unto you and to your fathers for ever and ever:

"And go not after other gods to serve them, and to worship them, and provoke me not to anger with the works of your hands; and I will do you no hurt.

"Yet ye have not hearkened unto me, saith the LORD; that ye might provoke me to anger with the works of your hands to your own hurt.

"Therefore thus saith the LORD of hosts; Because ye have not heard my words,

"Behold, I will send and take all the families of the north, saith

22 The Bible, Micah 6: 6-8 King James version

the LORD, and Nebuchadrezzar the king of Babylon, my servant, and will bring them against this land, and against the inhabitants thereof, and against all these nations round about, and will utterly destroy them, and make them an astonishment, and an hissing, and perpetual desolations."[23]

Such pronouncements in time of war skirt close to treason.

"Therefore the princes said unto the king, We beseech thee, let this man be put to death: for thus he weakeneth the hands of the men of war that remain in this city, and the hands of all the people, in speaking such words unto them: for this man seeketh not the welfare of this people, but the hurt.

"Then Zedekiah the king said, Behold, he is in your hand: for the king is not he that can do any thing against you.

"Then took they Jeremiah, and cast him into the dungeon of Malchiah the son of Hammelech, that was in the court of the prison: and they let down Jeremiah with cords. And in the dungeon there was no water, but mire: so Jeremiah sunk in the mire." [24]

Yet, Jeremiah is still considered a prophet and the words he presented as the voice of the Lord were duly recorded in the Hebrew scripture. Many of the early prophets were killed for precisely the same reason as was Jesus. They denounced the corruption and threatened the power of those who controlled the religious system.

Let us now turn to the man who, more than any other, shaped the theological system which created the Christian religion, Saul of Tarsus. Saul was a first Century Jewish Pharisee who became the Apostle Paul after his religious experience on the Damascus road. It was Paul's interpretation of the fact of Jesus' life and, most especially, the fact of his death, which formed the basis of the Christian message

23 The Bible, Jeremiah 25: 4-9 King James version
24 The Bible, Jeremiah 38: 4-6 King James version

and allowed it to spread in the gentile world even as it was stifled in its birthplace, the Jewish world. It is ironic that Paul's effort to place Jesus within the framework of Jewish theology, and thus make Jesus acceptable to Jews, was the very thing that exacerbated the theological split between Christianity and Judaism that continues to this day, with all its terrible consequences.

Much of Paul's conception of Jesus, and his shaping of Christian doctrine, hinges on his portrayal of him as the Jewish Messiah. In the first Century, the Jewish world was very much alive with the expectation that a Deliverer would soon appear. At that time, it was fervently hoped by all believing Jews that a descendent of David would come to restore his throne, throw off Roman suzerainty, restore Jewish national glory and make Jerusalem a "city on the hill" that would become an example and provide leadership to the entire world forever after. There was also the idea that the Messiah would usher in a new age, one in which Jewish Law and even death itself would be transcended. This concept is especially evident in Paul's portrayal of Jesus as the "new Adam."

Paul interpreted Jesus as the Messiah who transcended death and thereby provided a bridge to eternal life, a restoration of Adam's immortal state before the Fall, and naturally, the greatest longing of humanity. Jesus was also portrayed by Paul as the perfect sacrifice for the appeasement of God, thus rendering the sacrificial system of Judaism obsolete. As to the expected temporal deliverance of the Jewish nation, Paul interpreted those events as postponed until Jesus' promised return, which he and most early Christians were convinced was imminent. This contributed to the urgency and vehemence of Paul's efforts to convince the Jewish community that Jesus was the Messiah.

As explained in a remarkable little book by Richard L. Rubenstein, *My Brother Paul*, the Apostle never stopped thinking of himself as a believing Jew and was respectful of tradition even as he preached the radical overthrow of the Law because that overthrow was itself a part of the rabbinic Messianic lore.

Rubenstein is careful to portray Paul as a man of his day, who lived at a time when Jewish religious fervor was high and the people sought Messianic deliverance of the nation as well as the individual. Then, it was sincerely believed that "the sins of the father are visited on the sons" and that the Jewish people were suffering under Roman rule as payment for the sins of their ancestors. They believed that mankind as a whole suffered death as payment for Adam's transgressions. The message of John the Baptist, "Repent, for the kingdom of God is at hand!"[25] resonated with a people who believed that if every individual were purified, the nation as a whole would find miraculous deliverance and a new age would dawn as prophesied.

> "And in the days of these kings shall the God of heaven set up a kingdom, which shall never be destroyed: and the kingdom shall not be left to other people, but it shall break in pieces and consume all these kingdoms, and it shall stand for ever.[26]

> "I saw in the night visions, and, behold, one like the Son of man came with the clouds of heaven, and came to the Ancient of days, and they brought him near before him.

> "And there was given him dominion, and glory, and a kingdom, that all people, nations, and languages, should serve him: his dominion is an everlasting dominion, which shall not pass away, and his kingdom that which shall not be destroyed."[27]

Naturally, at the time there were various interpretations concerning the expected coming of the Messiah and the Messianic age as there were about other religious matters. According to Dr. Rubenstein,

> "In Paul's time the Jewish world was divided into a number of sects, each of which claimed that it alone was faithful to God's word as revealed in Sacred Writ. Today, the heirs of the Pharisees have won the spiritual battle within Judaism; their interpretation of Judaism is regarded as authentic and normative. The Pharisees were already exceedingly powerful and influential in Paul's day, but they were by no means unchallenged.

25 The Bible, Matthew 3:2, King James version

26 The Bible, Daniel 2:44, King James version

27 The Bible, Daniel 7:13-14 King James version

Then, rejection of Pharisaism was not equivalent to rejection of Judaism. Other groups, including the followers of Jesus, considered themselves loyal and faithful Israelites, although they offered competing interpretations of God's covenant with Israel. Paul offered one such interpretation." [28]

Though Jesus referred to himself by the name "Son of Man," which was associated with Daniel's Messianic prophesies, he never referred to himself explicitly as the Messiah. Nor did he make any move whatsoever during his lifetime to create a political organization in order to restore the throne of David. And even though Jesus used the term "kingdom of God" and prayed, "thy kingdom come, thy will be done on earth as it is in heaven," the term Messiah in the traditional Jewish sense could only mean one who actually effected the establishment of a political, as well as spiritual, reign. Therefore, Jesus *could not have been the Messiah.*

It is possible, however, that eventually he might have been accepted as a prophet by the Jewish people had it not been for Paul's insistence on their acceptance of Jesus as Messiah and all that then applied to the Messianic age which he insisted had dawned – especially the abrogation both of the Law and of the established system of sacrifice. Writes Rubenstein,

"Even in his radical reinterpretation of Scripture, Paul was indebted to his rabbinic teachers. His belief that Scripture could only be understood in the light of the Messiah's career was in some respects derived from the rabbinic doctrine of the twofold Law. According to the Pharisees, the true meaning of the *written text* of Scripture could only be apprehended in the light of their own interpretive traditions, which they designated as the *oral Law.* They insisted that the written and the oral Law were completely in harmony. However, they were frequently at odds with the Sadducees, who contended that the written text alone yielded an authoritative understanding of God's will. Thus the Sadducees rejected the doctrine of the resurrection

28 Rubenstein, Richard L., *My Brother Paul*, Harper Torchbooks, Harper and Row, 1972, pgs. 116-117

of the dead because they saw no evidence for it in Scripture. In contrast, the Pharisees interpreted the Law by means of their oral traditions so that it yielded the doctrine of resurrection... When Paul contrasted the letter and the Spirit of the Law (II Cor. 3:6), he was pursuing an interpretive strategy that had been suggested by his rabbinic teachers.

"By interpreting Scripture in the light of their own experience, the Pharisees made it a living document for their community while preserving a sense of continuity with the past. *This is exactly what Paul, the former Pharisee, did in the light of his own experience.* Paul's vision of the risen Christ became the prism through which all of life took on new meaning. He never asserted, "I reject the Law and the covenant because of Jesus Christ." The sacred traditions of his people never ceased to be divinely inspired for the Apostle. His problem was that of harmonizing a tradition he regarded as holy with his own experience. Things would have been very different had Paul really thought of himself as an apostate or believed that he was creating a new religion. He did what any other religious Jew at the time might have done had he been similarly affected. Admittedly, Paul's experience involved so radical an alteration in his spiritual cosmos that the new meanings he ascribed to Scripture seemed to his former peers and their successors to be a total rejection of Israel's sacred traditions."[29]

Rubenstein's interpretation of Paul is expressly psychological and specifically Freudian. He sympathizes with Paul's rejection of the Law because he himself struggled with maintaining a minute compliance, and in trying to achieve the "correct relationship with God," experienced nothing but frustration.

The fundamental issue at hand is actually the nature of God. If God is capricious in his wrath, and after all, the crime of Adam seems very slight in comparison with his punishment (along with the punishment of all mankind), coupled with the idea that one cannot know

29 Rubenstein, Richard L., *My Brother Paul*, Harper Torchbooks, Harper and Row, 1972, pgs. 117-118

which rules God values over others, it is therefore important that all the laws be followed lest one break a seemingly minor law which results in a breach in relations that cannot be repaired. In this view, man is forever in suspense as to his standing with his heavenly Father.

In the traditional Jewish view, God is indeed man's father, but a father who seems to delight in infanticide and this concept makes it very difficult for man to trust, much less to love God, even though it is commanded him to "love the Lord thy God with all thy heart, and with all thy soul, and with all thy mind, and with all thy strength."[30]

Rubenstein, along with Freud, contends there is an unconscious desire on the part of man to kill God the father in order to usurp his position, to become God, in other words. This certainly seems to be born out in the modern world with the rise of science along with the death of God as the seeming key to man's growing omnipotence. Perhaps the view of man as parricide is the psychological mirror to the idea of God as infanticide.

Rubenstein asserts that the fundamental problem for Paul, as for all men, is how to achieve the correct relationship with his Creator. Rubenstein explains that since it is impossible for man to truly identify with God, who became utterly transcendent with the fall of Adam, the Jewish answer is to obey God's Law as the only known method of fulfilling his will. Rubenstein surmises that Paul solved this problem by identification with Christ, the perfect, obedient son. Rubenstein views the consuming of bread and wine, symbols of the body and blood of Christ, as evidence of this need for primal identification. In this light, he also asserts that baptism may be viewed as symbolic of death and rebirth as a new member of the Christian brotherhood, again identifying with Jesus's death and resurrection. Paul seemed to have been of this opinion. Originally, this spiritual brotherhood was visualized as the body of Christ with Jesus as its head, but of course as time went on, the church and its teachings became the head. Thus the Church, in effect, replaced the "kingdom of heaven" in Jesus's teaching.

In accordance with Messianic prophesy, Paul envisioned the kingdom of heaven as an earthly estate. He proposed that Christ, as the new Adam, would remove the original curse of post-Adamic man, mortality, and there would be a bodily resurrection of the dead on

---

30 The Bible, Mark 12:30 King James Version

earth. Here it is important to remember the earth-centered cosmology of the time. Earth was conceived as the literal center of creation – the only stage whereon the cosmic drama could unfold. And as Christianity gradually transcended and absorbed the cult of Mithras which was popular in the Roman world at the time, it also absorbed the Zoroastrian concept of Good and Evil being locked in mortal combat. This undoubtedly shaped and influenced the apocalyptic ideas that became attached to the awaited return of Christ.

If we examine the concept of the "kingdom of heaven" that Jesus actually taught, however, we come away with a very different perception. Jesus seemed to propose the kingdom as a state of awareness that could be entered into *now*. Never did he say, "the kingdom of heaven will be like," rather said he, "the kingdom of heaven *is* like..." He described the conditions for entrance: to "become as a little child," that is, to accept one's relation to God as his child, and to be "poor in spirit," to be humble. Jesus's life may be understood as that of a man supremely conscious of his relationship with God and he taught that this acceptance of man's supreme relationship with God is what transforms life into the "kingdom of heaven."

Jesus illustrated the kingdom of heaven as an overwhelming awareness of its supreme value - the value of knowing and experiencing one's true relationship with God. In his parables, he describes the obtaining of this great value as worth the sacrifice of all else (the treasure hidden in the field, the pearl of great price). This experience of one's relationship with God transforms all else, (the leaven in the meal, the salt of the earth). It bestows the ability to separate value from non-value (the wheat and the chaff; the sorting of the fish). It is a value that grows of its own accord (the mustard seed); and is a gift that is bestowed rather than earned (the workers in the vineyard, the prodigal son).

This relationship with God, taught Jesus, is one to be accepted through faith, rather than achieved through obedience, and in this Jesus may be seen as radically re-interpreting the Law, but not necessarily overturning it. When arguing with the Pharisees or Sadducees over some minor infraction of the Law, Jesus always framed his argument in terms of value.

"What man shall there be among you, that shall have one sheep, and if it fall into a pit on the Sabbath day, will he not lay hold on it, and lift it out? How much then is a man better than a sheep? Wherefore it is lawful to do well on the Sabbath days."[31]

"Not that which goeth into the mouth defileth a man; but that which cometh out of the mouth, this defileth a man … For out of the heart proceed evil thoughts, murders, adulteries, fornications, thefts, false witness, blasphemies: These are the things which defile a man: but to eat with unwashen hands defileth not a man." [32]

"Ye fools and blind: for whether is greater, the gold, or the temple that sanctifieth the gold?" [33]

"Cleanse first that which is within the cup and platter, that the outside of them may be clean also." [34]

"Ye blind guides, which strain at a gnat, and swallow a camel."[35]

When viewed in this light, the work of Jesus falls much more in line with the traditional Jewish idea of a prophet than that of the Messiah. Jesus enlarged the concept of God and clarified man's relationship with him. He did not, however, fulfill the temporal mission of the Messiah and therefore it is right and correct that the Jewish people, in accordance with their traditional understanding of who the Messiah is and what he will achieve, should reject Jesus as such.

One need not accept the Messianic concept of Jesus in order to devote oneself to his teaching or even to accept him as divine. In this way, Christians may one day accept the Jewish rejection of Jesus as the Messiah without resentment and with complete understanding. And Jews may someday re-evaluate the life of Jesus and how his teaching fits

---

31 The Bible, Matthew 12:11-12 King James version

32 The Bible, Matthew 15: 11, 19-20 King James version

33 The Bible, Matthew 23:17 King James version

34 The Bible, Matthew 23:26 King James version

35 The Bible, Matthew 23:24 King James version

in with that of the prophets without the pressure to accept him as the Messiah.

Following in Richard Rubenstein's footsteps, let us extend our sympathy and understanding to Paul, but let us also admit he may have been wrong; that the kingdom of heaven may not be a future earthly estate, but a present spiritual one, to be entered into by humility and grace. Then the "old things are passed away; behold, all things are become new."[36]

Although, as Dr. Rubenstein noted, Christians take the word of Jesus as their highest religious authority, whatever Christians believe Jesus to be, should not preclude Jewish scholars from studying his work and his role in the Jewish tradition. Though there has been some work done to place Jesus in his historic context (Joseph Klausner and Bruce Chilton, for example), there has been no real systematic study by Jews of Jesus' religious work.

Perhaps they may in time reconsider Jesus' placement in the line of Hebrew prophets.

---

36 The Bible, Corinthians 5:17 King James version

9

Religion & Secularism

Returning now to the problem of Islam in the present context, there are many who argue that Islam need not be countered in its religious aspects, but only as a political system, because only by its politics are non-Muslims directly affected. In this view, the religious aspects of Islam are a private matter and should be of little concern. But as I have noted many times, a man's belief, that is, his fundamental view of reality, determines his attitude toward and reaction to the world of reality and to other human beings. Thus, belief systems must be of utmost concern if one cares about the destiny of humanity.

We abandon our responsibility to our fellow human beings if we do not address Islam in all its aspects. As Ibn Warraq has noted many times, "Muslims are the first victims of Islam." And though Islam certainly provides a strong sense of belonging which benefits social cohesion, it does so at the expense of personal freedom and individuality. Islam is something one is born into and cannot leave without the most extreme intellectual, emotional and physical struggle – a struggle very few win, as witnessed by the tiny number of ex-Muslims compared to the number of ex-Catholics or ex-Lutherans, for example. The right to question and leave the religion one is born into, is a fundamental freedom absolutely denied by Islam, which is why the numbers of Muslims multiply rapidly compared to other religious groups. In Great Britain, the Muslim population is multiplying at a rate ten times that of the rest of society. [1] Thus, curtailing Muslim immigration must be a part of the strategy of resistance. We have to deal with Islam as a whole and realize that it spreads not so much by the attractiveness of its ideas, but in large measure by simple procreation.

Religion in its most basic sense is what man perceives the nature of reality to be. Even the viewpoint that reality is impersonal and indifferent may be said to be "religious" because it is fundamentally a

---

1 Kerbaj, Richard, "Muslim population rising 'ten times faster than rest of society,'" *London Times*, Jan. 30, 2009

belief. It is religious belief which provides a common consensus about the nature of the world we inhabit and which forms the basis of culture. It is obvious that we in the West no longer agree on the basic nature of reality and thus our culture, which is at bottom a creation of the mind, is disintegrating. Here, Richard Weaver avoids the word "religion" by substituting the term "metaphysical dream," but his meaning is the same:

> "The darkling plain, swept by alarms, which threatens to be the world of our future, is an area in which conflicting ideas, numerous after the accumulation of centuries, are freed from the discipline earlier imposed by ultimate conceptions. The decline is to confusion; we are agitated by sensation and look with wonder upon the serene somnambulistic creations of souls which had the metaphysical anchorage. Our ideas become convenient perceptions, and we accept contradiction because we no longer feel the necessity of relating thoughts to the metaphysical dream.

> "It must be apparent that logic depends upon the dream and not the dream upon it. We must admit this when we realize that logical processes rest ultimately on classification, that classification is by identification, and that identification is intuitive. It follows then that a waning of the dream results in confusion of counsel, such as we behold on all sides in our time. Whether we describe this as decay of religion or loss of interest in metaphysics, the result is the same; for both are centers with power to integrate, and, if they give way, there begins a dispersion which never ends until culture lies in fragments."[2]

On the other hand, disintegration also comes on the eve of new creation: the seed must die before it can sprout. And though the old is passing away, disintegrating, something new may emerge as a center of integration. What may now be discerned is there is a new religious basis is in active formation centered on individual subjective experi-

2 Weaver, Richard, *Ideas Have Consequences* (The University of Chicago Press, 1948) pgs. 20-21

ence (God-consciousness) rather than theology. Theology is created by the reasoning made possible through anchoring thought in religious assumptions. But, as Weaver points out, the ultimate source of that anchoring is intuition, that is, experiential knowing through contact with reality.

As I have pointed out, a major element of confusion in both Judaism and Christianity is the failure to differentiate the very old conceptions of God from more modern conceptions. This has created a schizophrenic world-view in which God (or reality, or the universe – these may be used interchangeably) is both benevolent and malevolent at once. On the one hand, God is a loving, forgiving, transcendant and perfect father, but on the other, he is a stern punisher, chiefly concerned with making black marks in one's book of life and planning for one's eternal punishment in a humanly vengeful fashion.

Fear of God was the prime motivating factor for the religious person of olden time: "Fear of God is the beginning of wisdom."[3] Now, however, the motivating factor of both Christianity and Judaism seems to be guilt, or the avoidance thereof. It may plausibly be put forward, that the religious stream of the West is gradually moving away from fear as the primary motivating factor for religious living, through a period where conflicting ideas about the nature of reality are accepted. Ultimately, however, these conflicts must be resolved and religion must make sense to the modern mind.

Since the Enlightenment, Western man has, in large measure, rejected the schizophrenic view of God provided by Judaism and Christianity and opted instead for a God of indifference, or the idea that God is dead, or even that he never lived. In the extreme version of this view, the universe is seen as totally mechanistic and thus purposeless, mindless and valueless. Mind is nothing more that a glandular illusion and value is merely a social consensus which may change with the passing fashion. The great error here is the failure to differentiate the tangible from the intangible, between matter and life, or even between matter and mind. Samuel Butler's early and profound critique of Darwin rested upon his objection to the banishing of mind from the equation.

Materialism in the West hit its high-water mark no later than

---

3 The Bible, Psalm 111:10 King James Version

the first half of the twentieth century, when Jacques Barzun and Richard Weaver made their heroic efforts to reinstate mind as a reality to be reckoned with on its own terms. Their work stands in stark contrast to the increasingly insipid appeal of the new scientism which offers a chemical answer to every mental and emotional question.

The Muslim religion as we have seen is more or less comprised of an enhanced materialism. It might almost be described as materialism *as* religion. And as stated earlier, religion for Muslims is thought to be as much a line of descent as a set of beliefs, conferring as it does a belief in essential superiority.

> 'Since Islam regards non-Muslims as on a lower level of belief and conviction, if a Muslim kills a non-Muslim...then his punishment must not be the retaliatory death, since the faith and conviction he possesses is loftier than that of the man slain...'Islam and its peoples must be above the infidels, and never permit non-Muslims to acquire lordship over them."[4]

Like Western materialism there is no effort to differentiate the tangible and intangible in Islam. Worship itself is brought down to the material level, being thought of as the equivalent of obedience to Islam. And since Muslims are mainly created by being born into the religion, it is difficult to see much difference between Islam in this regard and the belief in Aryan superiority or the belief in the aristocratic superiority of an earlier age. The arbitrary idea of superiority outrages the overwhelming human desire for fairness. Islam is a man-made house of straw and will undoubtedly be destroyed by that unseen wind, the pressure of true proportion, measure and value, which is felt by all who love freedom. For it is clear, Islam unfairly enslaves the body, mind and spirit of all its adherents and therefore must be opposed in its entirety, as a religion, by religious counter values. If we attempt to oppose it as a political system, by political counter-values, we must confess our political values are ultimately rooted in religious values, just as in Islam and we are immediately face to face with the religious conflict we had hoped to avoid.

---

4 Tabandeh, Sultanhussein, *A Muslim Commentary on the Universal Declaration of Human Rights*, 1970

Perhaps the religious thought that will prove most effective in opposing Islam, is not the Christianity of the Middle Ages, nor the Judaism of Moses and the Torah, but a new and living religious sensibility based on the reality of the steady God-consciousness of those who have found their own personal religious experience. While it is tempting to dismiss the New Age movement as a fad, it nevertheless reveals a profound spiritual hunger and a widespread searching after a religion of experience in the West. Many, very many, are seeking and finding. Modern man desires his religion first hand, and is unsatisfied with the second-hand religion of the past, religion that is based on the experience of others, even if that "other" is Saint Paul himself. And herein lies a paradox, that the greatest objective reality (God) may only be found in a purely subjective manner.

"Then one of them, which was a lawyer, asked him [Jesus] a question, tempting him, and saying,

Master, which is the great commandment in the law?

Jesus said unto him, Thou shalt love the Lord thy God with all thy heart, and with all thy soul, and with all thy mind. [*Deuteronomy* 6:5]

This is the first and great commandment.

And the second is like unto it, Thou shalt love thy neighbour as thyself. [*Leviticus* 19:18]

On these two commandments hang all the law and the prophets." [5]

Truly this is the kernel of Western religious thought. In order to know God, one must love God and when one loves God, one partakes of his nature and it becomes impossible for the God-knowing man not to love his brethren, the children of God, even as God himself loves

---

5 The Bible, Matthew 22 35-40 King James version

them. Once a man discovers the kingdom of heaven within his heart, the world is transformed and all life is infused with new meaning and value. He cannot help but reject a view of God contrary to the loving spirit he knows by and through his own experience.

It is, however, all but impossible to oppose the twisted value system of Islam, by affirming there are no values except those of man-made consensus. One may point out the man-made nature of Islam, its essential materialism, its distortion of the scripture and the base character of its prophet, but one cannot effectively counter the God of Fear with a God of Nothing. The God of Fear can only be vanquished by a God of Love and to do this, love must be affirmed as the highest reality known to man. This cannot be done by an atheism that rejects the separation of matter and value, thus rejecting the reality of value, the reality of love, and the reality of the transcendent entirely. Religion can only be opposed by religion and it is to those God-knowing men who simply know that they know, who will most convincingly reject the Islamic characterization of God and its distorted world-view.

Throughout the twentieth century and into the first decade of the twenty-first, the life sciences have increasingly been devoted to examining the traits and characteristics man shares with other animals. The trend has been toward minimizing man's unique qualities and magnifying man's animal nature. The theory of natural selection, coupled with sexual selection is now being stretched to explain all aspects of human behavior and psychology. This has the effect of diluting the concept of will, and ultimately, of denying the non-material aspects of human experience entirely, including the reality of mind itself.

Thoughts are conceived as consisting of nothing more than electro-chemical processes taking place in the brain, and therefore, indistinguishable from it. The mind is said to present an illusion of non-materiality and abstraction which is, in fact, created solely by the material organ. The only way man differs from other animals comes down to the relative amount of grey matter contained within his cranium in comparison with his body mass. The fact that man has a larger and more complex brain is presented as the only difference distinguishing human beings from other animals, a difference which explains all others, including the creation of art, culture and religion.

This emphasis on the corporeal has effectively excluded metaphysical discussion from the public sphere. However, it is doubtful that the problem of "what is man?" can be fully understood without some discussion of the abstract. Certainly man differs from the animals in his ability to *self-reflect*. Animals may make and use tools, they may cooperate in groups, they may show loving care for each other and may even use language to a limited degree, but they cannot reflect upon their lives, or ponder the meaning of their existence or the reality of death.

The highest forms of human self-expression; art, music and literature, are not possible for animals because they do not have the capacity for self-reflection. Nor do they possess the capacity to imaginatively put themselves into another creature's place. The lion does not reflect upon the plight of the gazelle and indeed the entire animal kingdom is a strictly amoral abode on that account. There is no higher value for an animal than purely selfish survival and reproduction. Therefore, if we attempt to strain the arts through a materialist sieve, we are likely to remove the object of art which lies in the expression of higher meanings and value contained in mind and spirit. Viewing art as an evolutionary adaptation implies a strictly material benefit and while those benefits might be demonstrable, especially upon consideration of sexual selection, the overall effect of such theorizing is the unfortunate cheapening of the arts, even by those who desire to uplift and uphold them.

Coming at the problem of art from a metaphysical perspective throws a different light on its reality. Metaphysics releases man from pure materialism, in which there lies no inherent meaning – survival and reproduction are not meaningful in themselves if they do not relate to something higher. However, if one considers that the *patterns* to which all matter adheres, stable and yet flexible patterns, from the pattern of atoms, to the patterns of the elements and molecules, to the patterns of cells and life forms up to and including patterns of behavior, all may be considered as *mind* (not simply as described by mind), then we can begin to discuss the non-material as an element of reality, even as a reality itself. Simply put, natural law is pattern and pattern is mind. Instinct could then be considered a result of the interaction of living organisms with mind which produces discrete patterns of behavior, the seemingly miraculous "knowing" of animals.

If we consider mind a level of reality and that language and mathematics are patterns of mind, not simply "tools" human beings use to describe reality, man is thrown into a different relief with regard to that reality. Unfortunately, however, the prevailing notion that all reality is material, and *only* material, holds even the finest minds of our generation in its grip. They then seek after material causation for mind and value, which is the ultimate in reductionism.

In discussing the metaphysical, non-material aspects of existence, we may postulate that man has access to higher realms of mind than animals do, realms containing language and mathematics, which allow him a degree of freedom from the material, even from time itself. We may speculate as to whether man broke through into the higher realms of mind in a purely spontaneous fashion, or whether some event was an antecedent cause, but clearly what we are discussing is not simple animal-level consciousness, but consciousness *of* consciousness and that is one very real difference between man and animal. It is a difference that cannot be explained on a purely material level. How can matter be conscious of itself without the addition of mind and how can mind be conscious of itself without the addition of something even higher?

For most natural philosophers, the difference between man and animals seems to be purposefully blurred. It is simply assumed that the man is nothing more than an animal, and such differences as there are, are only a matter of degree. When forced to deal with something as basic as the value of art, many of these philosophers simply ignore it. Stephen Jay Gould, for example, explains art a by-product of evolution with no inherent evolutionary value. Denis Dutton takes issue with this in his interesting book, *The Art Instinct*. Dutton seeks to explain art as an important evolutionary adaptation in itself and succeeds rather well in arguing the case, at least for fiction, although in order to do so, he is forced to argue the point that the purpose of storytelling is to allow entry into the minds and experiences of others, something absolutely impossible for the animal mind to accomplish.

With his deep and wide knowledge art, literature and music, Dutton fully acknowledges the existence of beauty and love in human experience, though not necessarily as values with a separate existence in reality. The argument that man created mind, value and God in general seems quite settled now that the dogma of natural philosophy has come to dominate philosophy as a whole. Yet one must keep coming back to the question of what happened during the Pleistocene to turn a highly intelligent, tool-using animal into a being conscious of his consciousness, with the ability to reflect on his life and deeds and possessed of the added ability to discern truth from falsehood, goodness from evil, and beauty from ugliness? The entire history of man is one of fleeing the "red in tooth and claw" animal world and of protecting himself from its brutality by adding layer upon layer of culture. Culture is the creation of imagination. Animals cannot create culture because they cannot enter into the same levels of mind human beings do in order to perform feats of imagination.

In this respect, language must certainly be considered essential to the human condition, and again we may speculate that, metaphysically, language exists within that higher realm of mind which impinges on the realm of value (goodness, truth and beauty). *"In the beginning was the Word, and the Word was with God, and the Word was God."* [6] The power and mystery of language certainly go far beyond its dull utilitarian purpose of merely describing the material world. And yet, modern linguistics seems doggedly determined to study language on that dead level. And yet, it is undeniable that language (along with mathematics) bestows upon man the ability to be creative himself - to create his own reality, at least in some measure, rather than to simply exist as a part of creation. Language and will are thus indissolubly linked.

The concept of moral will lies at the very heart of human dignity. Yet we are witnessing a systematic attack on language as a moral instrument and an effort to remove all terms of judgment - to wring the life from language, so to speak. Words are powerful things and when employed in the service of higher value, they are very powerful indeed. Many of the same people who would remove value judgment from our language would also have us believe that Jesus (the ultimate teacher of the word) was nothing more than a schizophrenic homosexual in order to try to remove the power of his words from our minds. But what is it that distinguishes man *more* the power to make moral decisions?

In *The Ethics of Rhetoric*, Richard Weaver argues that it is impossible to remove all tendency from language, that language always tends to one direction or another, and that the effort to scour language of its moral tendency is nothing less than an attack on humanity itself.

---

6 The Bible, John 1:1, New International version

The modern obsession with genetic causes of behavior is perhaps the most overt of the modern attacks on the human will, but is only a part of the growing movement toward the reduction of man. In this, the modern secular movement is in line with Islam. For both, free will is nothing more than an illusion and morality is entirely arbitrary.

Science does well to purge religion of superstition, but it does not do well when it attempts to prevent humanity from exploring or understanding all non-material aspects of reality completely. Over the last century, secularism, which had originally blessed mankind by limiting the earthly power of religious authority, has gone far beyond that mandate and launched an attack on the reality of all that is non-material - on mind and value. Thus, secularism has evolved into an attack on humanity - on all that distinguishes man from animal. Even the finest minds of our generation have become enslaved by a dogma as strong as any religion, but one that is ultimately much weaker. For although Darwinism may explain from whence we have come, it is powerless to show us where we should go. We cannot discuss what *should be* without admitting the supremacy of value.

10

The Progressive Diminishment of Man

It may be argued that what man believes himself to be determines not only his conduct, but the substance of what he feels is possible, thus determining the scope of art and culture. The ostensible purpose of science is to serve man through the ever-expanding knowledge of facts, and yet as science has ascended, many scientists have mounted a purposeful attack on the ancient concept of man in order to diminish him in his own estimation. The feeling among scientists seems to be that man does not deserve a privileged place in the universe.

In the space of a few short generations, man has descended from seeing himself as a little less than the angels to king of the beasts to nothing more than a complex machine. The effect this has had on culture, on art and literature, has been devastating. For as the essential importance of man has decreased, so has his ability to portray life in anything other than absurd terms. In literature the concept of tragedy, which once hinged on the idea that the individual loss of freedom was of tragic proportions, has been all but lost. In Shakespearean tragedy, for example, a character flaw often compelled the central character to follow a predictable, tragic fate. But even in Shakespeare the idea of the hero, so prominent in Greek tragedy, was already diminished. Satire remained, of course, and continued from Pope through Byron. Then, in the 19th Century, we witnessed the rise of the psychological novel which then waned as the anti-hero rose to dominance. Today, literature has been reduced to a prolonged and tedious exploration of the aberrant. The hero has long been vanquished, with the exception of children's comic books, because man no longer sees himself in a great spiritual struggle with eternal stakes. Even that last bastion of heroism, the military, has reduced the description of its mission to nothing more than a "job." Indeed, the importance of human life has been so reduced that certain philosophers argue, with dead seriousness, that it is actually immoral to prefer human life over than the life of an animal.

The high priests of scientism, from Stephen Hawking to Richard Dawkins, argue that given enough time, science will eventually answer all questions, and implied is the idea that science, and science alone, contains all truth. However, upon examination, we find great areas where science has already abdicated. Science cannot, for example, explain the difference between a living and a dead organism in purely scientific terms. Scientists observe the elliptical movements of the planets and the mathematical precision of the orbits of electrons around the atomic proton, and postulate the existence of forces to explain these motions, but they cannot tell us what these forces actually *are*. For example, science can describe the effects of electricity, but it cannot tell us what electricity *is* any more than it can tell us what life is or what gravity is. It can describe the patterns of atoms and molecules, but it can no more predict that one hydrogen and two oxygen atoms combined would create water, any more than it could predict that the proteins in a DNA molecule could control the development of a living creature. As Ludwig Wittgenstein explained,

> "The whole modern conception of the world is founded on the illusion that the so-called laws of nature are the explanations of natural phenomena.

> "Thus people today stop at the laws of nature, treating them as something inviolable, just as God and Fate were treated in past ages. And in fact both were right and both wrong; though the view of the ancients is clearer insofar as they have an acknowledged terminus, while the modern system tries to make it look as if everything were explained." [1]

Darwin once famously asked, why thought, "being a secretion of the brain" should be considered "more wonderful than gravity, a property of matter?" Though thought, like gravity, is non-material, both, according to Darwin, can be safely assumed to be the products of matter. The secret of atomic organization and the organization of life, according to scientism, is thought somehow to be contained in the smallest dead particles of mindless material. Yet when we look at real-

---

1 Wittgenstein, Ludwig, *Tractatus Logico-Philosophicus*, (1921, translation by C. K. Ogden 1922) 6. 371-2

ity, we must admit that matter without pattern would remain undifferentiated and therefore it is pattern which is the determining factor, not matter alone. And if pattern does not exist in mind or as mind, then where does it exist?

It is literally true that we live in a world composed of pattern. One does not see the wind, but we see the effect of it; we do not see mind, but we certainly see its effects in the observable patterns of reality. To attribute complex patterns or even simple patterns to mysterious mindless forces only deepens the mystery rather than clarifying it. The fact that mind is non-material does not mean it is not real.

The human genome has now been found to contain a comparable number of genes as any other vertebrate and this is evidence that our bodies are no more complex than that of a dog or an ape. Yet this discovery hasn't prevented the proliferation of "scientific" theories about the genetic basis of language, art and culture. Language alone, with its well neigh infinite complexity, were it genetically based, would logically require an immense amount of genetic space. And if language cannot be found in our genes, how could art or culture be found there?

On the other hand, if we propose that mind is an element of reality, then we can reasonably assume that language can be found in its patterns. It may also be postulated that if mind exists as a level of reality, that its properties may gradually be discovered by man (as with the discovery of mathematical principles), but it would not be entirely accessible by any one man at any one time. If mind were simply the creation of the brain, it would, like the brain itself, be entirely subject to scientific inspection. On this subject, Noam Chomsky writes:

> "The greatest defect of classical philosophy, both rationalist and empiricist, seems to me to be the unquestioned assumption that the properties and content of the mind are accessible to introspection; it is surprising to see how rarely this assumption has been challenged, insofar as the organization and function of the intellectual faculties are concerned, even with the Freudian revolution. Correspondingly, the far-reaching studies of language that were carried out under the influence of Cartesian rationalism suffered from a failure to appreciate either the

abstractness of those structures that are "present to the mind" when an utterance is produced or understood, or the length and complexity of the chain of operations that relate the mental structures expressing the semantic content of the utterance to the physical realization.

"A similar defect mars the study of language and mind in the modern period. It seems to me that the essential weakness in the structuralist and behaviorist approaches to these topics is the faith in the shallowness of explanations, the belief that mind must be simpler in its structure than any known physical organ and that the most primitive of assumptions must be adequate to explain whatever phenomenon can be observed. Thus, it is taken for granted without argument or evidence (or presented as true by definition) that a language is a "habit structure" or a network of associative connections, or the knowledge of language is merely a matter of "knowing how," a skill expressible as a system of dispositions to respond. Accordingly, knowledge of language must develop slowly through repetition and training, its apparent complexity resulting from the proliferation of very simple elements rather than from deeper principles of mental organization that may be inaccessible to introspection as the mechanisms of digestion or coordinated movement." [2]

And again, when we discuss the "mental structures" of language we are discussing properties and patterns that exist in mind, not in matter. And for those who counter that mind is the result of brain-as-computer, one need only to point to the infinite complexity of language and how deeply and individually creative it is – the focal point of freedom and will. It is exactly that freedom and will that is under assault by the use of concepts like "cognitive systems" as though mind were a dead product of dead matter without the spontaneity or creativity of life. These explanations, for the thinking person, simply will not do, as Chomsky explains:

2 Chomsky, Noam *Language and Mind* (Cambridge University Press, Third Edition, 2006) pgs 22-23

"It is important to bear in mind that the creation of linguistic expressions that are novel but appropriate is the normal mode of language use. If some individual were to restrict himself largely to a definite set of linguistic patterns, to a set of habitual responses to stimulus configurations, or to "analogies" in the sense of modern linguistics, we would regard him as mentally defective, as being less human than animal. He would immediately be set apart from normal humans by his inability to understand normal discourse, or to take part in it in the normal way – the normal way being innovative, free from control by external stimuli, and appropriate to a new and ever changing situations.."[3]

One might recall the great glee with which Jane Goodall's discovery of the tool-making and using of chimpanzees was greeted (wild chimps were observed stripping the leaves from twigs in order to use them to fish for termites). This was due not to the fact that it raised chimpanzees in our estimation, but rather because it lowered man. Louis Leakey exclaimed, "Now we must redefine tool, redefine Man, or accept chimpanzees as humans." One more supposedly unique human attribute was knocked off the list, and we could no longer claim to be the only tool making and using animal.

Despite the best efforts of science, however, language has proved a much more stubborn human attribute. Animals can be taught to use language to a limited extent. My African Grey parrot can tell me what he likes and wants, "I like corn. I like peppers. Mommy, give me almonds," etc., but he can't enjoy what we would recognize as a normal human conversation. Chimpanzees and gorillas have been taught sign language, but with the same disappointing results and despite all the excitement and promotion of the possibility of language use among dolphins, it has never been found.

Animals can learn cause and effect and therefore ask for things, but human language is not so much about *things* as the *idea of things* and normally takes place on a level above; concerning itself with the relationship between the ideas of things. This is what renders meaning.

3 Chomsky, Noam *Language and Mind* (Cambridge University Press, Third Edition, 2006) pg. 88

Mind as it is experienced, can be divided into various levels. The level of mind that concerns itself with perception, the recording of perception, motor control and the involuntary nervous system is undoubtedly connected with the material brain and is shared with animals. Animals are also undoubtedly conscious, but human beings are conscious of being conscious. This implies a level of mind experience above that of animals. Add to that the ability to use language and to explore levels of meaning through the use of language and mathematics and we have yet another level of mind which animals simply do not experience.

Though there is nothing to be gained by denying this obvious reality, it is my contention that even the possibility of exploring the non-material realm of mind has been effectively blocked by the overwhelming consensus of modern science that we live in a meaningless material universe and only the weak-minded would say otherwise. It is because science has progressively diminished man in his own eyes that philosophy has been stunted. We stand dumb in the face of confident Islamic assertions because we long ago abandoned the search for an effective and modern philosophical response to materialism. Islam is, in essence, an extremely materialistic religion with many similarities to secular materialism: both remove human dignity and envision man as a slave. And while our politicians continually exalt the concept of freedom, our philosophers going back through Spinoza to William of Occam and the rise of nominalism deny there is any such thing as true free will.

The current materialist vogue of dismissing the reality of the non-material amounts to an attack on the reality of mind. For example, in *How the Mind Works*, Steven Pinker condescendingly asks,

> "How does the spook interact with solid matter? How does an ethereal nothing respond to flashes, pokes and beeps and get arms and legs to move? Another problem is the overwhelming evidence that the mind is the activity of the brain. The supposedly immaterial soul, we now know, can be bisected with a knife, altered by chemicals." [4]

4 Pinker, Steven as quoted by Marilynne Robinson in "Thinking Again," *Commonweal* May 7, 2010

Therefore, each human being creates his own "mind bubble" of experience, and therefore psychology, not to mention morality, is reduced to a series of electro-chemical "flashes, pokes and beeps" in the individual brain and the mental process, that is to say our thoughts, may be controlled, and perhaps one day entirely controlled, by chemical means.

The modern scientific tendency to explain all experience in material terms has engendered a marked hostility toward any experience not so readily explainable, especially that of the value-realm, love, or even what one might term "religious experience." Today, such life-changing occurrences are likely to be diagnosed as schizophrenic delusions and anti-psychotic medications quickly prescribed rather than to be taken seriously as actual, meaningful, personal experiences. As Thomas Scheff explains,[5] this labeling (diagnoses coupled with drug treatment) creates social isolation of the patient which reinforces his feelings of disconnectedness and confusion which may in turn prolong the mental crisis and even turn it into a chronic state of psychological dysfunction. When one considers that often these crises are the result of an initial spiritual experience (which can cause temporary disorientation) we begin to see a tendency to isolate and medicate those with the wrong ideas. Spiritual birth can sometimes be quite traumatic, but when it happens in a society that labels this kind of sudden awakening as mental illness, it can be devastating, even life-threatening to the individuals involved.

Scheff contends that recovery from psychosis is directly related to the patient maintaining a connection with at least one other person through a loving relationship[6] – someone who sticks with him through thick and thin. Psychiatrists, however, generally put a tremendous amount of pressure on the patient to remain on anti-psychotic drugs, drugs that can be extremely debilitating. This reinforces the idea that the person is "sick" and "different" not simply experiencing something extraordinary or going through a psychic reorientation as a

5 Scheff, Thomas J. "The Concept of Normalizing: Neither Labeling nor Enabling" *New English Review*, June 2010
6 Scheff, Thomas J, "Instances and General Ideas: Parts and Wholes" *New English Review*, April 2010

result of an extraordinary experience. In a footnote, Scheff states that "the biography (Nasar 1998) of John Nash, a Nobel Prize winner… shows that Nash's mother and wife aided his recovery, since they never gave up on him. However, *A Beautiful Mind,* a film purportedly based on Nash's biography, misinformed on the drug issue. Nash, played by Russell Crowe, attributes his complete recovery to 'the newer antipsychotic drugs.' But the biography states that Nash refused to take drugs after 1970, long before the newer antipsychotics. Indeed, the biographer states that his refusal may have been fortuitous, making possible his complete recovery (1998, p. 353)." [7]

Less dramatically, the everyday religious experience consists of the discovery and progressive realization of values – truth, beauty and goodness - their combination in love and activation in service. Values are first experienced and then the reasoning mind seeks their explanation through theology and philosophy. There is no more striking evidence of society's hostility to religion than the fact that the psychiatric profession considers strong or extraordinary religious experiences as psychotic delusions and actively isolates and medicates a certain percentage of those who have trouble processing those experiences.

In the world-view of material determinism, there is no place for the concept of free will, and therefore not only is it entirely inadequate as a source of explanation for the human condition, materialism poses a real danger to personal autonomy and freedom. It is a reflection of the extreme arrogance of modern man that he would turn on that faith which sustained his ancestors for centuries and label religious individuals "crazy." Psychologically speaking, there may always be an urge among the young to turn against the old order, the "father" of their existence. According to Sigmund Freud, the urge toward parricide runs through religion from its earliest inception,[8] and in a certain sense, this latest effort to destroy God is also a religious act, though unrecognized as such.

In essence, two different methods exist for seeking reality. One is entirely external (the realm of science, materialism) and the other,

---

7 Scheff, Thomas J. "The Concept of Normalizing: Neither Labeling nor Enabling" *New English Review,* June 2010

8 See Rubenstein, Richard L. "There Is Nothing Final About The Death Of God" *New English Review* April 2010

internal (the pursuit of values, or religion). And even though there is evidence philosophy is beginning to regain its former role of reconciling and balancing these two methods, the last century has been entirely dominated by the former. As Stephen T. Asma wrote in *The Chronicle Review*:

"No self-respecting professor of philosophy wants to discuss the soul in class. It reeks of old-time theology, or, worse, New Age quantum treacle. The soul has been a dead end in philosophy ever since the positivists unmasked its empty self-referential center. Scientific philosophy has shown us that there's no there there.

"But make no mistake, our students are very interested in the soul. In fact, that is the main reason many of us won't raise the soul issue in our classes: The bizarre, speculative, spooky metaphysics that pours out of students, once the box has been opened, is truly chaotic and depressing. The class is a tinderbox of weird pet theories—divine vapors, God particles, reincarnation, astral projections, auras, ghosts—and mere mention of the soul is like a spark that sets off dozens of combustions. Trying to put out all these fires with calm, cool rationality is exhausting and unsuccessful." [9]

Such efforts are ultimately doomed to fail because of two experiential factors. One is the direct experience of value and the other is the unmistakable feeling or sense that the body is not all that we are, even that the body is a thing apart from our true selves. The experience of value is not the result of reasoned deduction. We may deduce that something is relatively true through the use of reason, but the experience of the light of Truth, like that of Beauty or Goodness is just that – an experience. The aspect of personal reality which directly experiences value is something we call the soul. By this we mean the realest and truest part of ourselves and to deny its reality feels something like a betrayal.

---

9 Asma, Stephen T., "Soul Talk" *The Chronicle Review* May 2, 2010

One might even question whether it is at all reasonable to deny the reality of value-feeling any more than it would be reasonable to deny the reality of sight or sound. Though one cannot transfer religious experience from one person to another any more than one may see through the eyes of another, it is the height of arrogance to assume that because one has not experienced something that another has not experienced it either. It is worse to assign what may be the most meaningful experience of a person's life to the effects of cerebral dysfunction. It may certainly be argued that those who embrace the experience of value lead more meaningful and well-adjusted lives than those who deny that reality and who attribute the experience of God-knowing to the effects of neuronal misfire. To those who proclaim "you do not know," the believer can only respond, "how do you know I don't know, and furthermore, who are you to deny my experience?"

So because true religion ultimately rests upon personal experience, it is not something that lends itself readily to debate. Though points of theology, philosophy and religious history may be challenged and altered through time, the experience of the believer stands apart. The experience of soul growth, that is, the process of assimilating or identifying with truth, beauty and goodness and thereby feeling one's soul become increasingly real is not something that can be objectified, despite the assertion of Pinker cited above, because it is an entirely personal experience. Nor is it something that can be altered with the latest fads in psychology, religion or science, though all these things may color and shape how these experiences are interpreted.

When we contemplate how our rapidly decaying culture might be revitalized, the obvious solution is through religion, the ultimate basis of culture and the source of cultural nourishment. Yet religion cannot be revived by appeals to the past, no matter how scholarly, noble or erudite ancient thinkers were. Religion has to be restated in modern terms that make sense to people steeped in scientific reason. We can't simply retrace our steps and return to the Age of Faith. A new religious understanding must be born, shorn of superstition, and respectful of science, but not subservient to it. A strong reassertion of the reality of the non-material, the reality of mind and of transcendent value along with the reaffirmation of personal religious experience and personal autonomy will go a long way toward reclaiming the foundation of religious faith which has the power to solidify social unity. We may disagree on points of philosophy or on solutions to a myriad of social problems, but if we can find a unity of spirit and agree on the general direction of what "should be," then we can also find the strength to defend those cultural values we hold most dear, including freedom of expression and freedom of true worship.

The reinvigoration of Western culture must include the restoration of man to a place of dignity in a meaningful universe. The first step must be to restore mind to a level of reality, not illusion, otherwise meaning and values cannot be considered to be real. If mind is not real, then all of man's knowledge and all his finest accomplishments in art and science are as nothing and the Muslim designation of the fruits of our culture as worthless *jahiliyya* would be justified. Perhaps it is time to revisit the works of Kant, Descartes, Aristotle and Plato and recognize that the banishment of mind from the realm of reality has not necessarily been wise. For without mind, where is will? and without will, where is freedom? Let us restore man to his proper and dignified place in a meaningful and thus mind-filled universe. One may even assert that in mind, we live, move and have our being.

11

Why Islam is Not a Religion

Over the years since the September 11 attacks, when describing Islam, many political commentators employ words like radical, political, extremist or militant as qualifying adjectives or they use the words Islamism or Islamo-fascism in order to specify their criticism is of the political side of Islam and are careful to exhibit no hostility toward Islam as a religion. This approach caters to the prevailing political orthodoxy by implying that there is an overwhelming majority of Muslims devoted to the good religious Islam with only a small subset of extremists fighting for the bad political Islam, which most Muslims themselves don't necessarily endorse. We call this the "two Islams formula."

Politicians love the two Islams formula, in fact, both administrations since 9/11 have subscribed to it, because it means they don't have to do anything about the spread of Islam. Muslim immigration, mosque building, Islamic schools, proselytizing in our prisons and military, and the infiltration of our institutions by Muslim Brotherhood front groups all go untouched. Politically, we are limited to fighting terrorism and terrorist financing and that is it. Not surprisingly, the Muslim Brotherhood loves this formulation and actively promotes it as well because it gives them religious cover for everything they do. We must recognize that the actual imposition of Shari'a law is the final stage of Islamization. So if we aim our attack on Islam's legal system alone and leave unquestioned the status of Islam as a religion, we will find the battle lost before it begins.

To examine this question we have to look at religion as a whole. Religion is the most powerful force in human affairs. Religion is the prime mover because religion forms the basis of a shared worldview. From this basic worldview grows culture and from culture societal structures are formed and the final fruits of this process are political systems. Our culture, social affairs and politics are ultimately anchored in morality and morality is anchored in the basic world view derived

141

from religion.

Religion answers the primal question, what is the nature of reality? Do we inhabit a benevolent universe, a malevolent universe, or an indifferent universe? This is not trivial question and its answer determines the basis of all human interaction. At this primal level, as the creator of a distinct world-view which forms the basis of culture, Islam certainly qualifies as a religious system.

But we must also examine how religion functions in society; what religion does or ideally what religion should do. The following categories may not perfectly fit every religion, but they are broad enough to cover Hindusim and Taosim on the one hand and Judaism and Christianity on the other.

1) Religion must exalt value. It must constantly point toward truth, goodness and beauty and their combination in divine love as the highest reality. Religion must exalt value above matter and physics, above mind and logic, above all other perceived reality. This is not to say that religion is irrational, it is not, but spiritual reality as it is perceived in the form of truth, goodness and beauty must be exalted as the ultimate source of order, therefore, logic cannot supersede value. In other words, truth must measure the content of mind, not mind the content of truth. This is the essence of religious thinking. When the human mind becomes the measure of all things, we have left the realm of religion and have entered the realm of ideology.

In addition to elevating the will of one man to divine levels, Islam actually denies the reality any value higher than Islam itself. Islam essentially acts as a substitute God because it is presented as the will of God for all mankind for all time. Religion, as normally conceived, regards the will of God, outside a few general moral injunctions, as a matter for each individual to discover. In Islam, the "will of God" is a set of rules governing the most minute and personal aspects of behavior. Furthermore, Islam continually elevates the material over the spiritual, so much so, that values are essentially blocked from the consciousness of many Muslims. For example, as quoted in chapter one, the following are the words of the father of a failed female suicide bomber:

> "If I had known what [my daughter] was planning I would have told the Jews. I would have stopped her."

And of course the interviewer is thinking, the man loves his daughter and any person would be appalled at indiscriminate mass murder. Who wouldn't have tried to prevent such a tragedy? But then the father goes on to explain why he would have stopped her:

> "In our religion it is forbidden for a girl's body to be uncovered even at home. How could a girl allow her body to be smashed to pieces and then collected up by Jews? This is absolutely forbidden."

Mass murder is not the issue. His daughter's suicide is not the issue – the issue is the purely material matter of her body parts lying uncovered in the street for strange men to see and then being collected by Jews, which, since Jews are in the same unclean category as feces and urine, defiles them further and brings a double shame on the family. The dead and maimed are beside the point. This is an extreme example, but it is part of a pattern that is repeated in Muslim countries all the time. Islam comes first, life comes second and matter is elevated over value.

2) Religion must advance morality, and it must do so both for the individual and for civilization as a whole. Because for all the material advancement of civilization – advancement in science, advancement in technology and the advancement in material comfort - one must still ultimately measure the advancement of civilization by its moral progress.

Islam retards morality not only by elevating a set of arbitrary rules above spiritual value as we have just seen, but also because Islam lacks a true guiding moral structure.

All human beings are subject to pressure from two poles of passion broadly described as sentimentality on the one hand and brutality on the other. Between those two poles lies culture, which informs us how we should feel and should conduct ourselves in any given set of circumstances. Culture lends refinement to our emotions and informs and enforces self control. There can be no culture without self-control.

The skeleton of culture is morality - the enjoining of that which is *right*. Without a cultural morality requiring self control, man lurches from sentimentality to brutality with nothing between to balance or to refine emotion. This is exactly what we see among Muslims. They seem to lurch between weeping over dead babies on Al Jazeera to beating up their wives and children with no self-control whatsoever. Islam enforces self-control only in the sense of conformity to Islam. This is often disguised as moral consciousness, especially when forcing conformity on women, but is it? Obviously, conformity and morality are not the same thing.

Islamic morality collapses in on itself because it is based on two things: 1) expediency (that which is good for the Muslim community is *good in itself*) and 2) the word and deeds of Muhammad (whose words and deeds were often immoral). So, without a true moral structure to uphold it, Islamic culture collapses into barbarism and Muslims themselves exhibit an extreme emotionalism lacking all self-restraint.

Of course this very emotionalism is what causes the authorities in the West to treat Muslims like children who cannot be expected to exhibit self-control.

Culturally speaking, though Muhammad is claimed to be the final prophet in the Hebrew line, he certainly cannot be said to have advanced morality beyond the point where Jesus and the olden prophets left it six hundred and fifty years earlier. In Islam, morality is defined as obedience to Islam and therefore the higher moral nature of Muslims is suppressed and even denied, because again, in Islamic thought, there is nothing higher than Islam.

3) Religion must nurture the individual and help him pursue the higher values, which is the ultimate goal of religion. All true religion fosters righteousness, the desire for truth and the sensitivity to beauty in the individual. The goal of religious living is the attainment of those values as living realities in one's life.

The individual is sacrificed at every stage of his life for the sake of Islam. All of life is thought to be a test of the willingness to sacrifice happiness (which means, in effect, the pursuit of truth, goodness and beauty) for a promise of life in the hereafter. The exercise of individual freedom and the pursuit of value through either the questioning of Islam or leaving Islam are both viewed as treason and are punishable by death. That way, ideas dangerous to Islam are not spread among the collective – which is often described as one body. In Islam the collective is always elevated above the individual. The rough edges of individuality must be suppressed in order that Islamic society will run smoothly. We can see quite clearly that for women, at least in public, individuality is entirely erased by the veil.

4) Religion must preserve wisdom. Words of the God-knowing men of the past must be preserved for those seeking spiritual guidance in the present and future. Both Judaism and Hinduism have preserved religious documents for thousands of years. No easy feat before the time of the printing press and other technical advances we take for granted now. Today, religious wisdom is in danger of being lost in the general crush of information and entertainment, so religion's task may be even harder today.

Islam defines everything existing before the coming of Islam as the time of ignorance. The wisdom of old is therefore rejected and destroyed whenever possible. In addition to religious works, this includes cultural artifacts, art, literature and music.

Islam, as we know, claims to be an Abrahamic religion and yet has thrown out all the literature preserved by the other two genuine Abrahamic religions, Judaism and Christianity, which in itself should disqualify it as an Abrahamic religion. It would be like a church claiming to be Christian while throwing out the New Testament. Despite the fact that this makes no sense whatsoever, everyone from the Pope on down seems to accept the claim that Islam is an Abrahamic faith without question.

Muhammad made his claim to be the last of the Hebrew prophets, the seal of the prophets in fact, by advancing the idea that he was descended from Abraham through the bastard line of Ishmail and co-opted the legend that Hagar and Abraham journeyed 750 miles through the desert on foot with a baby to Mecca even though there is absolutely no independent historic substantiation of this at all. There is, however, a record of the descendents of Ishmail remaining in the area of Hebron in the Bible. It is recorded that Ishmail attended his father Abraham's funeral there, which is another reason why the Bible is rejected by Islam.

According to the Bible, Muhammad absolutely could not be the final prophet in the Hebrew line. The Jews of Medina are on record as having pointed this out, which is why Arabia is Judenrein today and Islamic antisemitism persists.

5) Religion must foster peace and social harmony. The promotion of empathy, tolerance and forgiveness among individuals, along with a sense of universal brotherhood is one of the most important aspects of religion.

Islam is a recipe for perpetual war. Not only does Islam divide the world into the believers vs. non-believers who known as the "enemies of God," but there is also perpetual warfare within Islam as well. Samuel Huntington called this the bloody borders and bloody innards of Islam. In the newspapers everyday we witness the fact that on average, more Muslims are killed by their fellow Muslims than non-Muslims are killed by Muslims and this despite the fact that around two million south Sudanese Christians and animists have been killed by Muslims in the last two decades. As Bill Warner has estimated, in the last 1400 years, Islam has caused the death of 270 million people and counting. With the destructive potential of the weapons they are quickly acquiring, it would not surprise me if another 100 million are added to that total in this century.

6) Religion should strengthen the family by promoting mutual love and respect between a man and woman who come together to build a home for their children. The nuclear family is the basis of all our social institutions and is the primary institution through which our cultural values are transmitted from generation to generation.

Islam destroys the family through the adoption of polygamy. Polygamy is not marriage. It degrades women and promotes inequality between the sexes. Do we want our daughters to grow up in a world where little girls are worth less than little boys anywhere in our society? Furthermore, wherever polygamy goes, child abuse follows. This is true of Mormon polygamists as well. [1]

7) Religion must hold to the transcendent purpose of reconciling man to a greater reality - it must lead man to God and bring God, or Love, if you will, into the life of man in ever increasing measure. Religion must always stand apart from the social and political institutions of the society in which it exists. Its function is not to uphold the status

---

1 See Bynum, Rebecca "Polygamy and me" *New English Review*, April 2006

quo, its function is to show man a higher reality.

One of the most important points to make about Islam is this: the purpose of Islam is only found in the perpetuation of Islam. Islam literally has no higher purpose. It sacrifices human beings on the alter to itself and for no higher purpose than to spread Islam.

So though Islam resembles a religion superficially and harnesses the religious impulse for its own perpetuation, the case can be made that Islam is not a religion in any meaningful sense. Ask a Muslim a spiritual question and you will receive a material answer. If you ask a Muslim, "What do you believe in?" The answer will be something like, "We believe you have to pray five times a day, fast at Ramadan, go on the hajj to Mecca" and so on. And if you press the point, you will get a lot of detail about each ritual. "First you have to wash, first this foot then that foot then this arm, then that arm, then this nostril then that nostril…" The Muslim questioned may actually think he has explained his religion. If you persist and ask why a ritual is performed, you will get a story about Muhammad - Muhammad said so or that's the way Muhammad did it. Islamic rituals, elaborate as they are, have little or no symbolic meaning beyond that.

Just because Muslims themselves are convinced Islam is a religious faith, doesn't mean the rest of us have to accept it as such under our laws, laws that were meant to foster religions that exalt value, advance morality, nurture the individual, preserve wisdom, promote peace, strengthen the family and that have a transcendent purpose. If we remove, or at least call into question, Islam's status as a religion, it will allow us to deal effectively with Islamization by regulating immigration, mosque building, Islamic schools and proselytizing in prisons. The foiled synagogue bombing in New York demonstrates how serious the problem of prison conversion is and it will only get worse.

Scientology, for example, is not recognized as a religion in every nation and scientology, as far as I know, is not inherently seditious and a danger to the state and to our citizens the way Islam clearly is. In short, Islam is like the duck-billed platypus of belief systems and because it is so unique it deserves its own category – some Latin word combining politics and religion perhaps. But, even if we do not consider its political aspects when considering the status of Islam, I believe there is enough on religious grounds alone to disqualify it as a religion in the Western world.

Unfortunately, because Islam is presently classified as a religion, there are those who view the present Islamic assault as confirming all their worst fears and negative assumptions about religion in general and have taken up the ideological sword not just against Islam, but against all religion, especially Judaism and Christianity.

We are constantly bombarded with the chant that fundamentalist Christianity is just as bad as fundamentalist Islam, that Christians if they had their way would impose a theocracy on the United States and that the real danger to liberty in America comes from these Evangelical Christians. This has become the standard party line of the hard left who even liken Orthodox Jews in Israel to Hamas, as though they were morally equivalent. It seems that for many Jews, Israel is an embarrassment. And Israel, by insisting on its right to exist, is endangering all the rest of us and our comfortable, complacent lives. If Israel were to disappear, goes the thinking, all our problems with the Muslim world would likewise disappear.

If jihad is being waged on Israel, it is Israel's fault. If jihad is being waged on America, then obviously, it is America's fault. This, of course, is the argument of Islam – the infidel is always guilty. Because the hard left is always ready to view the Western world as guilty and responsible for all the ills of the rest of the world, they are already predisposed psychologically to begin the process of imbibing the dhimmi mentality, so eloquently described by Bat Ye'or in her pioneering work on Islamic history. The process has already begun.

The view that Christianity and Islam are ideologically close is supported by two factors. One is the fact that some Christians and most Muslims are united in opposition to the way evolution is taught in the schools. This alone leads many secularists to put Christianity and Islam together in the enemy camp. This view is also supported by the pervasive use of the word "conservative" to describe Islamic attitudes and nations, as though King Abdullah and William F. Buckley were ideologically aligned. In this view, conservatives are all enemies of progress, so if one believes in evolution and in progressive social change, one has no choice but to oppose both conservative Muslims and conservative Christians.

Secularism, however, as we have known it in the past has been characterized by indifference to religion. Its attitude was that religion and politics should be separate. But in recent years these self-described secularists have become much more radical and have turned on religion with surprising hostility and seem to be using the present crisis with Islam to hammer nails in the very coffin of God. But if one examines both Islam and the new atheist movement, it becomes clear that these radical secularists are actually much closer philosophically to Islam than either one is to Christianity or Judaism. It is no accident that both Islam and the new atheists are vehemently anti-Christian.

As described earlier, in Islam, God's will is defined both as the rules of Islam for humanity and as everything else that happens in reality. God's will literally controls everything and God employs evil as part of his work. There are elements of this kind of thinking in Judaism and Christianity as well, but not to the same extent and not as universally as is found in all schools of Islam. In fact, I believe the book of Job can be read as a criticism of this kind of thinking that ends with the creature becoming morally superior to the creator. In Christianity, God's power is not usually elevated over his love or his desire for our love to be freely given in return.

In Islam on the other hand, if the planes hit the towers, it was God's will, not the will of men alone. If a tsunami hits Indonesia, killing tens of thousands, that is God's punishment for not following Islam closely enough. Islam consistently reduces God's will to simple brute determinism and since nothing happens that isn't God's will, there is no difference between that and the idea that there is no God. God is force. And if everything is immediately, not just ultimately, predetermined, there is no free will for mankind – there is no choice to make between that which is God's will and that which is not God's will. According to Islamic thought mankind's only source of security is to cling to Islam in order to avoid divine punishment.

This is paralleled in the modern scientific idea of material determinism. According to this position, matter and force are all that make up reality. What we experience as mind is simply a "secretion of the brain" and what we experience as value is nothing more than the evolutionary genetic encoding of cultural convention which has allowed some groups a greater chance of survival over others. According to this view, even our virtues of duty, honor and charity are simply disguised selfishness. We are genetically predetermined to have such illusions as the values represented in art, literature and music. They give us comfort, but the ultimate value of virtue, or of value itself, is in the selfish genetic survival value it confers – there is no other value intrinsic in truth or beauty or goodness, for these things do not exist in reality.

Morality, then, is indistinguishable from conformity to the social mores just as it is in Islam. Islam has the advantage here because at least in Islam, morality, such as it is, is stable, whereas in the view of the material determinists, morality is merely an ever-shifting set of cultural conventions. Even our exalted ideal of human rights can be altered at the "drop of a law," to quote Theodore Dalrymple, because there is nothing higher than human will. Islam elevates the will of one human being to divine heights. The new atheists elevate their own in the same way.

Of course, we have seen the outworking of this kind of thinking before. America risked all to oppose it twice in the last century, but this time it is within, pushed by our Universities, and absorbed by our colleges, high schools and grade schools and it pervades society generally as political correctness and the smug self satisfaction of those who believe in nothing higher than themselves.

Like Islam, material determinism attacks the very core of our culture, the thing that provides what remains of integrative power, the common conviction that God exists, that he is good, and that we have the choice to become like him in a universe which is a benevolent place in which we belong. There is no greater integrating or unifying force than religion. Without religion, we have absolutely nothing with which to counter Islam. Muslims cry: we have the truth in Muhammad and the Qur'an. Materialists reply: there is no truth. Muslims are strongly unified in loyalty to their ideals and are willing to die for them. Materialists maintain there are no ideals worth dying for and all idealists are sentimental fools.

Islam and material determinism stand on either side of nihilism. Islam saves society from the anarchy inherent in its philosophy by imposing ultra-strict totalitarian social regulation. Material determinists promote the idea of a world shorn of all meaning and value, and imagine that society will be more peaceful, just and tolerant without them. Both break man down to the animal level, and thus both are fatal to civilization.

Civilization is the product of both morality and imagination: it represents the distance between human society and the jungle. We cannot maintain that culture, that imagination, as represented in art, music and literature by reducing man in his own eyes from something a little less than the angels to nothing more than a selfish brute, to a glorified material machine. The effect of this philosophy is evident in the overall decline in our culture, even as our technology, with all its creative and destructive power advances apace.

Materialists are systematically disarming the West ideologically and trying to remove the greatest source of its unity, its religion, and they are doing this now, at this most critical juncture the West has faced since the fall of Rome. Even the Soviet Union had the wisdom to re-open its churches during the war. It would be prudent to save this internal fight for another day, but prudence, unfortunately, does not characterize the new atheist movement.

Furthermore, given the depth of Islam's hold on the minds of men, the liklihood of the western world being able to secularize the Islamic world is slim to non-existent. It is much more likely that the secular world will become Islamized.

We are therefore facing an ideological war on two fronts. Islam has amply demonstrated its power of cultural annihilation, but so has material determinism. What was Nazism, but Darwinism taken to its logical extreme? What was communism, but the effort to create a totally rational society, shorn of all religion? The effect of both these ideologies was to destroy more human lives and possibly more civilizational potential than all the previous wars in history combined. Islam has certainly racked up its share in body count over the centuries and its effect on human creativity has been even more devastating. Those who care about art, science and culture, must oppose all efforts to remove the greatest source of both civilizational unity and the greatest font of civlizational creativity, our religious faith in the reality of transcendent value, our faith in the reality of God's Love.

Reverence for democracy and respect for secularism will not be enough. Only faith in a loving God and the conviction that truth, beauty and goodness are real can oppose faith in a God of hate, a God of untruth, ugliness and cruelty. Religion itself is not the enemy and should not be treated as such.

What we face is not only a clash of religions, or even a clash of civilizations, but a clash between levels of reality. Thus, we fight on the side of truth against error, goodness against evil, and life against death. The justice of our cause is self-evident: opposing evil is not evil. We stand upon a foundation of love in opposition to a foundation of fear and hatred. If we can hold the high ground, and deal with Islam firmly and with Muslims humanely, we will not lose.

Allah is already dead.